NO EXPIRY

A woman fights fear and ageism and takes on the wilderness…alone

Sheila Nollert

Sheila Nollert Publishing

Nollert, Sheila, 1957 –

No Expiry / Sheila Nollert

Cover photo: Stock Photo

ISBN: 978-1-7381337-0-3

DEDICATION

This book is dedicated to my husband, Tom, and my children, Bruce and Beverly. Their understanding and support of all my endeavours is unwavering and allows me to be unapologetically me. I have learned so much from each of you. I love you.

To my grandchildren; Brooklyn, Jeremy, Francesca and Zachary; may you grow up knowing that you can be capable of whatever you reach for and that you are never defined by age. Never forget that Grandma Sheila loves you.

To my community and followers on my Instagram @grandma_moves, thank you for the connection we share in promoting active aging. Your constant support drives me forward each and every day.

START HERE

It's difficult to follow your dream. It's a tragedy not to. ~ Ralph Marston

What is it that makes the distant hills call to us, the trail lure us to see what is just beyond the next bend or has us follow the sun, rushing westward even as it disappears, pulling up the night in its wake as it tucks itself below the horizon? There has to be something in our psyche. Was it when we were nomadic in nature and had to travel to find our food source based on the time of year? Is it a survival tactic, always exploring to see if we can find a better place that provides food, shelter and security? I can't tell you, but I know this feeling well. It begins as a simple thought - imagine what I could see from that hilltop, I want to chase the sun so it doesn't set, or, what special thing awaits me on the trail just out of sight? It only grows from there, expanding until my feet are trying to take me in that direction. It is a rising thrum in my heart…it is exhilarating. Not only that, but it fills some empty spot in my soul, makes me reach out to connect with nature, embracing her rhythm tightly so as to never lose it again. To me, this is life at its best, when worries fall away and there is only right here, right now to immerse in, and I drink it in like it is the nectar of the goddesses. Maybe for you it isn't the hills, trails and the sun, but perhaps growing flowers or your own food and nurturing it from seed to table, whether that be in a vase or on a plate. It could be that your spark is ignited by dragging photography equipment to the tundra and camping out in the hopes of capturing an elusive animal with your lens. We all have different things which give us this feeling – zest for life.

You know, we all experience pivotal moments in our life which become the impetus for change. At the time it happens we swear we will follow that path, achieve that goal, change our attitude, get that new job, whatever. Sometimes we

1

actually do it, other times, well, life happens and it is put aside. Time slips by and before we know it, nothing has happened, yet we yearn for something lost, something that seems just out of reach for us at this moment.

Does this resonate with you? It sure does with me. I have always loved the outdoors and came to canoeing and tent camping in my 20's when our children came along. Now the kids are gone with children of their own, and our tent camping has evolved. First, it was a small 16 ft travel trailer that stayed on site year round at Haliburton Forest and Wildlife Reserve on Kelly Lake until the kids were teenagers and no longer wanted to go camping. Then, when the kids grew up and there were again just the two of us, we bought a tent trailer that we used for a few years until in 2014 we bought a 25 foot travel trailer. I thought that was the full extent of our camping. I didn't even know I wanted more... or should I say, less, yet that's when a slow awakening over the course of four years occurred for me, culminating in a fantastic adventure in 2022 at age 65 when I went into the backcountry of Algonquin Park and completed a 4 day, 3 night solo canoe trip; paddling eight lakes, portaging my canoe and gear 14km through forest trails and sleeping in the wilderness each night, alone.

With this book, I hope to lead you gently into the realization that you can do things on your own and enjoy the magic that happens when you open up your bedroom door, from where everything is safe and cozy, and step into that large living room called your life. Pull open the blinds, let the light in and see, for the first time, what is really there.

Is there a time limit for this? Do we have to make certain we do the things that make us joyful before a certain age? Don't we get too old? I can tell you emphatically, the answer is no! We do not have an expiration date. While we may have limitations that warrant variations in the way we do these things that matter to us, we need only be creative. We must never utter the words "that ship has sailed". We must never give up. We must stay in the game.

It took mental work to get myself into the right mode required to make this trip happen. I am no different from anyone else out there who could come up with a million different reasons why this wasn't a good idea, and this is why it is important for you to read this book. You will see my process from start to finish, from overcoming those internal thoughts put there by society of "you're too old", pushing aside the skeptics, kicking fear to the curb, staying true to myself and acknowledging I completely had the ability to do this.

If you have some burning desire, regardless what it is, allow the spark to ignite, give it the fodder it needs to keep it going, let it grow into a fire, shape it how you want it to look, let it warm you. Remember the power of words; spoken inside our head or out loud. Words wield power. We know so much from watching body language, yet it's the words that can cut, soothe, give hope, drop us on the spot…and kill our dreams. Words change everything. Negative self-talk can stop us from achieving our goal and thwart our efforts making us feel like a failure and perpetuating more negative self-talk. This becomes our reality.

This is your one and only life. What you do with it is totally up to you. Live it as you wish, not for those well-meaning loved ones who may try and dissuade you. Remember, they are only worried about you. We cannot control or concern ourselves with how others will deal with the vision we yearn for. We need to trust they will manage just fine.

Afterwards, you will take pleasure in a sense of achievement that will course through your veins like effervescent life energy. Memories, vivid and colourful, will be yours to return to time and time again. Your life experience, the one you made happen, and there isn't anyone who can take that away from you. It's yours to keep.

So, if you are feeling the prickle of excitement beneath your skin as you read this, give audience to the lost intention which has been in the recesses of your mind, locked away safely 'for another day'. As long as we are capable, there is

Sheila Nollert

nothing to stop us. Certainly, and most importantly, neither age nor gender should deter us.

STAND ASIDE, I FEEL A MOOD COMING ON

And one has to understand that braveness is not the absence of fear, but rather the strength to keep on going forward despite the fear ~ Paulo Coelho

I know the first thing you probably might want to know is why. Why, at age 65 did I suddenly embark on a solo wilderness canoe trip? Did I fall down and hit my head, wake up with this silly notion in the same way someone hits their head and comes to with the ability to speak a different language they had no prior knowledge of? Well, no. It didn't happen like that. It had been there for some time, in the deepest recesses of my brain where there are drawers, mostly empty, some of which have never been opened and there's a constant echo in there, yet there was this folder called "Waiting for action" hanging around until I figured out which drawer to store it in. It sat most of the year unnoticed until the month of September when I once again found myself up north on our annual camping trip, standing on a shoreline gazing wistfully at the wilderness surrounding me and wanting, no yearning, to be there – out there, within the bosom of Mother Nature. I wanted to connect on a level I knew was there but I couldn't quite reach with the distractions of everyday life. That is when, every year, the folder was once again activated and put in the priority position of "Seriously waiting for action".

This wasn't something that had always been on my radar, but one year, in 2017, my husband, Tom, and I took our 25 foot trailer and made our way to North

Algonquin Park for the second time and this time while we were there, I watched a woman loading up her canoe with gear…by herself. I watched, waiting for someone else to appear – a partner or friend, but there was no one else. Where was the other person and why were they allowing her to do all the work on her own? She didn't seem annoyed to be doing it all herself – methodically placing and securing each pack in the proper spot, attaching her map to the thwart, stuffing a jacket behind the stern seat and lining up backpack pockets within easy reach. Then she simply got in the canoe and next thing I knew, she was paddling off down the lake, her canoe creating a gentle V in the calm waters of early morning, each stroke of her paddle taking her further from my view into the backcountry where she would have to carry her canoe and packs from lake to lake, over hills and rocks, quiet footfall through varied forests and meadows, and I found myself thinking this was the most amazing thing ever. I watched until she was just a speck on the lake and then nothing at all as she merged with the reflection of the forest along the far shoreline. I imagined what it might be like to be that speck disappearing and embarking on an adventure into the wilds. I was intrigued. I was in awe. I felt like it was the most beautiful thing I had ever witnessed.

That wasn't what did it, though. Let's just call that the seed of unintended desire, a desire I didn't know I had, and a spark flickered within. The following year, at the same campground, I watched a pink canoe come in from down the lake. A pink canoe! A woman from the U.S. was just finishing a 10 day trip in the backcountry. Solo. Gosh, this was a thing! But, a pink canoe! There's a 16 foot statement if ever there was one. Women are powerful. We can do things! Yeah!

I felt something then. That something you feel when you come to realize something exists that you had no idea about and it just happens to align with everything you believe in. Yes! The spark became a flame. That happened.

I took no action those first years, simply feeling the awe that these women were empowered to go out into the wilderness alone and camp night after night in their flimsy little shelter, immersed fully in nature and everything that entails, be it beautiful or scary as hell. It seemed enough for me...at first.

The following year, with our trailer set up at the same lakeside campsite, I excitedly watched for other women heading off on adventure. I wasn't disappointed. I watched a woman pack up her canoe; securing her well used gear to the thwart, stepping confidently into her craft and without a backward glance as she left the security of the campground, head out into the lake, small wavelets smacking the side of her vessel, her long, brown hair blowing free. Somehow I knew she was a minimalist. I felt a sisterhood. Later that afternoon when I spoke to Carmen Cross, who manages the campground, she acknowledged the woman actually described herself as a minimalist and after an absence from canoeing solo and tripping for several years, she was happy to be returning to it. The flame inside me grew.

It wasn't a week later that one night around 11pm, my husband, Tom, returned from walking the dog and told me he was pretty sure a woman who had just pulled into the campground parking lot was sleeping in her vehicle overnight. She had simply parked, then climbed into the back of her SUV. There was a canoe attached on the roof. There was no question in my mind this was a gal about to head out on a solo trip. I was very excited about the prospect of meeting her in the morning before the permit office opened.

As luck would have it, I did see her the next morning, carrying her canoe and gear down to the shore. I walked down, introduced myself, told her I was very interested in what she was doing, and asked her if I could bring her a tea while she waited for the office to open. Kelly was delighted I would make her a tea because she had decided not to bother making one for herself only because she didn't want to undo her packs, anxious as she was to get out on the water.

Kelly was embarking on a five day trip and this was by no means her first. She tripped solo regularly and got out whenever she could. When I told her how amazing this sounded and how I thought I would love to try it myself, she told me that of course I could. The words were easy enough to hear but my first thought was that I was quite a bit older. This was the thought that slammed the door on possibility before I even took the time to look to see what was on the other side.

The entire time she was gone, I thought of her… paddling long, narrow lakes, open bays, portaging all her gear on century old worn trails from lake to lake, finding a good spot to set up camp and sleeping overnight in the forest where I imagined fear of the unknown must be your constant companion.

Five days later, I watched for Kelly to return all day, my eye scanning the horizon repeatedly for any sign of a canoe, until finally, mid-afternoon, I saw her coming down the choppy lake churned up by a stiff west wind. Even though the wind was strong, she stopped paddling to take a last picture of the view before she came in to the shore. This gal was comfortable in her vessel. One with the elements. A wilderness warrior. Impressive.

I ran down to the shore and called out before she even hit land and as she gently nosed the canoe in to shore she had the biggest smile. At first I thought she was going to hug me. I felt it coming but then she changed her mind, probably remembering she was just back from 5 days out in the backcountry and thinking I wouldn't appreciate it.

Her hair was hidden away, wrapped up in a red bandana and crowned with a straw hat that had a fake pink flower limping sideways from it. She was annoyed because she had broken a thwart on her canoe. This happened when one of the lakes had a low water level this season and in order to get to the portage she had to plod through about 30 meters of knee deep mud and drag the canoe alongside her to get to shore. The thwart just couldn't take the strain. Even so, she just had a glow about her. Did hearing all this douse the excitement of me thinking perhaps I could do such a thing myself? No. It only made the flame of desire burn brighter.

Even so, as much as I wanted to, I didn't know how to get beyond the nagging doubts.

In the following days I went and talked with Carmen in the office several times about women who went out into the wilderness on their own. Carmen told me there were several every year, and more in recent years as opposed to twenty years ago when she first started at the office and it was a very rare thing to see. Every time we talked, I became more emboldened by the idea.

I suddenly wanted to talk to these women and find out why they did it. I wanted to know everything there was to know about it, and that evening when I sat on my favourite large rock just off shore to watch the sun set, I knew I didn't just want to talk about it. I wanted more than that. I really wanted to do it. The flame was a full blown fire now. My entire body resonated with excited energy.

That was the moment I first made the virtual folder, "Ready for Action".

Sitting on the shoreline our last night of camping that September in 2019, watching the sun slip behind the pines, I felt the peace of day's end descend. Overhead, birds travelled to their rest spot for the night, rose coloured sunlight catching their wings. I began to imagine what it would be like to do a solo trip. It felt intoxicating to think of being out there, in the belly of Mother Nature, by myself, experiencing everything first hand. Right at that moment, it didn't scare me. It warmed my soul.

As you well know, life happens, and in 2020 it happened big when the entire world was being held in abeyance as Covid 19 impacted us all in a huge and unprecedented way. The campgrounds were closed much of the year and even though they did open with restrictions later in the season, we didn't camp at all during that time. My "Ready for Action" folder lay dormant as I began to wonder if this solo canoe/camping trip into the wilderness was realistically something I could do. I was older than the women I had witnessed going out there, true enough, but it was the overnight I was most concerned with. I had to admit that sometimes just walking through the campground in the dark could be a bit scary, never mind being out in the middle of nowhere all by myself with no one else around. I began to have doubts and my fire flickered.

The following year, 2021, even though Covid 19 was still running rampant, the campgrounds were open. We were happy to get camping again and found that being in nature, you could forget the stresses the virus was causing worldwide. There was no one wearing masks, except at beaches where people were in closer proximity, and distancing was naturally occurring by fact everyone was on their own campsite. That September we were back at North Algonquin Park and as we pulled onto our site with the lake stretched out before us, the sun like shards of fractured light dancing across the water, my "Ready for Action" folder came to the forefront as, once again, I felt the wilderness reach out to me.

Even with all this waffling back and forth and thinking, yes, I am going to do this, it still wasn't a sure thing. On one of our camping trips that year, I was the object of a man's attention. He didn't do anything to me, yet it was obvious and unnerving. What made it scary was the way he was following me around even while Tom was nearby. On our last day there, he stole our registration form from the camp post which had our full name on it. Maybe it was the ongoing stress of Covid 19 along with the unwanted attention, I don't know… but I caved. I wasn't going to do that solo trip. How could I possibly go out into the backcountry and be so vulnerable if someone with bad intentions came along in a canoe when I felt like this at a campground with people about? What would I do out there? It really shook me up, and the cloud followed me home where I was watchful everywhere I went. He had our name so it was conceivable he might know where we live. Was this guy going to show up? What would I do if he did? I felt deflated and in a funk that I didn't know how to get out of. That inner flame of mine, once burning so brightly, was barely recognizable, all but extinguished - a warm ember with no energy to sustain it.

Finally, in March 2022, a friend said to me they understood why I felt the way I did, but reminded me that we only live once. I know this, of course. We all know this, yet I needed to hear it. It was a pivotal moment. I wasn't going to let this man extinguish my light and steal my power. He had already sapped months of my energy.

Basically, what it boiled down to was I simply had to do this, or live with regret and that inner voice – you know the one – "You can't do this". "You're too old". "You couldn't have even done it a few decades ago". "Let's get with reality"... Sadly, it is society's voice, too, once we reach a certain age. I was going to have to ignore the negativity as it served no purpose other than to immobilize me.

I was back on track. I was going to do my solo trip and I was going to do it that very year in September. The ember ignited into a flame larger and brighter than it had been before.

I'M DOING THIS THING

Believe in yourself. You are braver than you think, more talented than you know, and capable of more than you imagine ~ Roy T. Bennett

Now that I had made the decision I was going to really do this thing, I had to begin planning and commit in order to make it real otherwise the risk would be it may never happen. It was a mind thing. I knew I was totally capable of carrying the canoe and my gear over rocks, up steep hills and down again. There was nothing to stop me, other than my inner voice telling me I would be afraid at night. I would wake up in terror and not be able to go anywhere to feel safe. I knew this fear came partially from reading a young woman's account of what was to be her first night sleeping out in the backcountry alone. She paddled to her site. Set up. Everything was perfect. She laid down to enjoy the warm afternoon and fell asleep, waking up just as the sun was making ready to disappear over the horizon and dusk was about to descend. Knowing that the minute it was dark she would be stuck there until morning, she panicked and became overridden with anxiety, tearing down her tent and throwing everything into her canoe in order to get back to her vehicle, which was luckily parked on the same lake, just at the other end so there was no portaging she had to deal with. She made it back to her vehicle and now found herself again at square one, with the immediate desire to try again.

It isn't an easy thing to reconcile sleeping in the wilderness with the wild animals we know reside there who move stealthily under the cover of darkness. Even the scurry of a mouse can sound like you are surrounded by a pack of drooling, yellow eyed wolves flipping a coin to see who gets the first taste of your flesh, immobilizing you in fear, if you let it. I was determined I wasn't going to let it. I began a meditation practice in order to learn to control any anxious moments I may have.

The set up for doing such a trip was ideal. The Kiosk Campground exists as a jump off point for many canoe routes, so there were ample to choose from. Tom and I came to this campground every year at the same time for at least a two week period, so we would simply come as usual and during our stay I would head off right from the shoreline of the campground and return days later. I wouldn't have to drive anywhere so if it were the case I hadn't slept a wink the entire time I was gone, it wouldn't matter. I would just pull my canoe up on the shore, walk over to the trailer, tell Tom to go get the canoe while I fell into bed. It would never get more perfect than this.

Pulling out the map of Algonquin Park showing all of its canoe routes is always a time of excitement for a person such as myself who loves looking at maps, showing all the possibilities contained within - little red lines cutting across landmass connecting squiggly blue lakes embedded in an expanse of forest void of highways and any other signs of human habitation. Algonquin Park has 2400 lakes. We're talking options.

When I had the first ideas of doing this trip and I didn't have a clear vision of what it would entail, I initially decided in order to appease my less than excited husband I would spend my first night in the backcountry down and across the lake from the campground where he would be able to see my campfire and know I was okay. Then, the next morning when it was evident I hadn't been eaten by a bear and everything was going well, I would head off, leaving Kioshkokwi Lake behind…but to where? There were just so many canoe routes, so many loops…which one to choose? Probably the first trip should be kept simple in order to improve my chances of success. Maybe if I just had one long portage into Lake Lauder and set up for four days in one spot before returning, that would be the thing to do. It wasn't on a canoe route, simply being a lake unto itself at the northwest boundary of Algonquin Park. The reason this lake appealed was I had met a couple a few years ago returning from a back country trip where they spent four days on Lake Lauder and never saw another soul. Not one canoe ventured into the lake while they were there. What could be more amazing than having an entire lake to myself for a period of days? Trip reports online revealed a 1km portage that was flat and easy into the lake.

While the solitude of that sounded very nice, it didn't leave me quivering with excitement. It didn't feel too much of a challenge and I compared the long, flat portage to taking a two lane highway direct to my destination instead of a backcountry single foot trail winding through forests and meadows. If I was going to do this, I wanted to feel like it was indeed an accomplishment born out of skill, sweat and determination. I wanted to feel like the early people of this land did when they travelled between lakes through forests of dark green canopies segmented by bedrock, rapids and streams.

There were so many ways of going about solo canoe tripping and camping, all for very different reasons, but there was a common thread which bound them all – the love of nature and the joy of experiencing it alone – finding inner peace and leaving behind the routines we are bound to. Like so many things in life, there are many paths to a destination. You just have to find and do yours, not someone else's. I knew then I would be happiest if I went for it, portaging lake to lake, carrying my canoe and gear, setting up, taking down and having the full backcountry experience.

In the early days of preparation for this epic adventure before I even knew where I was going, I bought myself a GoPro7 to be able to record my experience. I barely had it out of the package to look at it, then sold it a few months later because I decided I did not want to experience my trip from behind a camera lens. To me, it would seem like watching it instead of being in it.

Another purchase I was initially happy about was a two person tent. I was practically ecstatic with how easily the thing went up, but I was not feeling warm and fuzzy about the tight space inside and found myself wondering where the heck I supposed to put my backpack. I am not a big person and yet there was no room in there. Realistically, I could leave the pack outside because there would be nothing in it to attract animals outside the tent any more than inside, but that isn't what I wanted. I wanted it inside, with me, where I could use it as a buffer in an emergency if a bear decided it wanted to sleep in a tent, too. I ended up selling that as well, after I had it too long to return. It seemed like I was aimlessly grasping at things to see what would stick – what would make the trip feel real. I was going one step forward, two steps back.

Tom was convinced the big four person tent we already owned would be good enough for my needs. There were some positives to this. I knew how it went up and it would save me tons of money. The not so positives were, it was heavy as a log at 4.5kg, and I thought it was quite old and a zipper may give out. In the end, the money factor influenced me and I decided to use it on the trip.

When you want to make a commitment and have a better than average success rate of it coming to fruition, you tell people about it. Now I had been telling a few people over the years I was going to do this amazing solo trip but this didn't do a thing to stop me putting it off again and again. I needed to go bigger and tell everyone I was doing this! Short of renting out a billboard alongside a 400 series highway in Toronto, I opted for a simpler, and cheaper, option.

In March 2021 I had started an Instagram account called @grandma_moves, posting every day, even over holidays save for the two weeks each autumn when we are in Algonquin Provincial Park and there is no cell service. The purpose of this social media account is to promote positive ageing through a healthy lifestyle, showing people the myriad ways they can move about to improve their situation through fitness. I decided to make my commitment with my followers as witness in May 2022 when I realized this was it. This was a big step. Was I going to tell them all in May that I was doing this in September, then change my mind and hope they forgot? Not too likely. So, I told them. I showed them my canoe. I flipped it over, lifted it and carried it over my head around the yard for them, grinning ear to ear. It was easy to feel invincible in the yard.

I did a few updates over the months, showing my equipment, telling them my plans as I made them. It served in making it real. To my surprise and delight, I got more excited as the weeks ticked by and my trip was getting closer and closer. I began to tell everyone about my plans, feeling confident this was happening.

When I began to make it public that I intended to do a solo canoe trip into the backcountry of Algonquin Park, portaging my canoe and gear through forests from lake to lake, camping out in my tent every night with no one to help if I needed it, I was inundated with comments. Some felt it necessary to immediately share the most spectacular bear attacks ever known to man, embellished upon with every telling, I'm certain. Most harboured skepticism hidden behind what they hoped were helpful comments of things I clearly hadn't considered, given my age and gender.

"Did you know they had to kill a large number of bears in the Algonquin Park last autumn because so many of them were becoming problematic to wilderness campers?"

"I heard a man was killed with one swipe from a bear when he came to the aid of a woman being confronted by one."

"I know a guy who told me the Ministry of Natural Resources released bobcats in Algonquin Park."

"I sure hope you have a gun!"

"You do know that wolves hunt people, don't you?"

"This might be the last time I ever see you…"

No Expiry

"Can you read a map?"

A concerned family member asks what I will specifically do if a bear decides to make itself apparent, coming into my campsite and showing no fear of me. My first instinct is to say I will throw my arm around its shoulders, give it a big kiss on the lips and invite it to stay for dinner, but instead I dutifully reply with what they want to hear, and that is I will be carrying bear spray.

The response wasn't good enough. They persist.

"What if that doesn't make it go away?"

"Then I will throw myself to the ground before its feet in the high drama I am capable of, tell it I am a grandmother to four lovely grandchildren and beg for mercy." I catch the words mere nanoseconds before they leave my lips. "I'll make lots of noise and make myself appear big…and nasty," I say instead.

"No, but what if it just doesn't want to leave? What then?"

"I'll get in my canoe and find another spot."

I see the start of what I know is the delivery of yet another question but I don't wait for it because, frankly, I am running out of answers. "Look, the worst case scenario, I leave my stuff behind, go out into the lake in my canoe and wait until I am certain it is gone, even if that means shivering all night out there on the water. "

All this bear talk doesn't go unnoticed by my psyche. I know there are bears. This isn't a revelation to me. I also know it is possible, yet unlikely, I will encounter one, yet now my inner voice demands to know precisely what it is that I think I am doing, going on this ridiculous trip at age 65. I could almost waffle – but I don't. This is important to me. The last thing I want is to be lying in a hospital bed, in failing health, unable to get up and realizing I will never again cast my shadow on the earth's surface, feel a squishy lake bottom ooze up between my toes or see stars like strings of lights between branches of trees. In reviewing my life, I don't want to be left thinking, geez, if I had only fulfilled my dream of solo tripping in the backcountry…

I have loved canoeing since I first tried it when our children were young. It's perfect for a gal like me who does not like speed, like that of a motorboat, or noise...like that of a motorboat... In a canoe, one can meander along the shoreline, gently steer around obstacles with a C-stroke or make a turn with a cross bow reach, feather into shore sideways by making a figure eight with the paddle or keep the vessel straight with a J-stroke...all without making a ripple in the water. A whole body experience. Nature resonates within your body rather than your body resonating with the vibration of a boat motor. This was my thing.

As a young family, we learned paddling techniques from the Barrie Canoe Club, a great club we belonged to for a few years. Tom and I even went on to take a weekend whitewater course with the club on the French River in northern Ontario on some rapids known as the "The Haystack". This was a valuable course, not because we ever planned to do whitewater, but to know what to do if we found ourselves in rapids inadvertently. It amazed me that you could finesse, ferry across, control and even eddy out of the rush of water to plan your next move – no screaming necessary. Full disclosure, I did flip the canoe in the rapids and experienced a moment of being stuck with my knees tucked under the front seat, my head beneath the water surrounded by agitating, wild froth and endless bubbles, confused as to which way was up, before being able to get loose as the canoe floated into the calmer waters below the rapids. It shook up the experienced paddler in the stern who was teaching me. He swam to shore and mechanically stepped out of the water up onto the rocks to his waiting and concerned wife, not once looking back to see me swimming after our paddles and struggling to turn the canoe over in shallower water.

We have two canoes at home. One is an older fiberglass 16 ft vessel, heavier than you can imagine. When we bought it, for the purpose of the whitewater course, it weighed 29.5kg It feels heavier now. It is beamy and as stable as they come, but I cannot carry it the distance I would need to on this trip. Tom bought me a new 16 ft carbon fibre canoe several years ago that I can lift easily and initially it was this canoe that I planned to take along on my solo trip. The canoe, a Swift

Prospector, is a thing of beauty and I love it. It looks beautiful out on the water – but there was a problem.

The thing about a very light canoe is if there is any wind at all, say goodbye. You're fighting it with every stroke and if you ease up at all, it turns you sideways and takes you faster than a blender to somewhere you don't want to go. It can be a struggle. I am speaking from experience. This was a little concerning because when you're out there you have to paddle if you want to get anywhere, so after further consideration and also envisioning the balancing of a 16 ft canoe overhead as I clambered over rocky trails and steep embankments, I justified renting a 13.2 ft Solo Pack canoe from Algonquin North Outfitters. After paying with the click of my mouse to secure the rental online from my dining room table one sunny April morning, I felt more committed than ever. This was really happening.

Next, I planned my route. I wasn't going to camp on the same lake the first night, and I wasn't going to simply portage into the next wilderness lake and stay in one spot for the duration. I was going to plan the route how I wanted it to look, and that meant three nights on three different lakes. Not having any idea how long it would take me to paddle these lakes, locate a campsite and set up camp, I selected a nice little loop that looked manageable, even though it entailed some longer portages. What made it even more alluring was that it was the very fact there were some longer portages on this route that it wasn't as popular as other routes. When I say I wanted to do this alone, I meant alone, not waving at 8 or 10 canoes throughout the day as I paddled the lakes.

Once the route was determined and the dates we were going to be at Kiosk Campground were booked, I could do my own booking and I reserved my wilderness overnight stays on the lakes I had chosen. Here, too, I recognized the ugly head that is ageism when I called the parks booking system to get assistance. I was having trouble and wanted to be certain I was doing it correctly. The employee who answered the phone was very helpful and pleasant and I was making good headway with her prompts…until I mentioned to her that I was

Kioshkokwi means "lake of many gulls" in Algonkin. The name holds true today.

Loop: Kioshkokwi, Little Mink, Mink Lake, Club Lake, Waterclear Lake, Whitebirch Lake, Little Mink, Kioshkokwi

"Erables" is French for "maples."

unable to see the senior rate on the drop-down menu. Regardless if it was intentional or not, and I suspect it wasn't, the change was immediate. She asked me if I would like her to finish the booking for me and it would only cost $2.00. I thanked her but said I preferred to know how to do it myself and was happy to continue as we were. Her patience seemed to disappear and a moment later she asked yet again if I would like her to complete the booking on my behalf. The thing was, it wasn't as though I wasn't understanding something. Often people assume an older person is incapable of understanding how to navigate online and use current technology. I ended up opting for the regular charge, foregoing the senior rate, even though it cost more than the $2.00 if I had allowed her to do it for me. It was the principle. Aside from this, it was an exhilarating time for me. I had put aside my dream year after year and now things were quickly happening…because I was making them happen. Finally.

My trip was still four months away, but honestly, I thought about it all the time. I ordered a new 75 litre backpack that had a great design of an additional zipper at the bottom of the pack enabling me to access items without pulling everything apart from the top. Plus the lovely burgundy colour was the bomb. It, too, was ordered online with a click and then all that was to be done was to wait for it to arrive on the porch. Gosh, I loved online shopping!

The food I would take on my trip had me thinking for a bit. I considered making my own and drying it myself, rehydrating it as I needed, but I couldn't shake a distant memory of when I had done that decades ago when Tom and I went with the Barrie Canoe Club on a weekend backcountry trip. I had dried the food and packaged it. When it came to dinner time, I added the water and we heated it up. It hydrated perfectly, but embarrassingly there was enough to feed a crowd. A very large and very hungry crowd... There was no use asking if anyone else in the group wanted some because everyone was already busy eating their own food. When you are out in the backcountry, you don't want food around that is going to attract bears and I did not have any container to put the extra into before hoisting it into a tree in our food pack. As we considered our dilemma, I had my eye on a dog someone had brought with them. It was so long ago, I can't tell you if it was a German Shepherd or a Husky, but it was a large breed dog. I went over to its owner and asked if it was okay if we gave it some of our leftovers. I remember the woman smiled, waved her hand in the air and said "absolutely!"

The dog ate the entire amount. I have no idea if that dog had the runs during the night, all the next day, week, month, but it was a lot of food. I was very grateful for that dog. I'm not convinced it would ever fall for that trick again if a similar situation presented itself.

It was for this reason, I decided I wasn't making my own dried food for my trip.

I wanted this trip to go as smoothly as possible so I could enjoy every minute and in preparation for how things might go out there, I booked three nights at Arrowhead Provincial Park in early June by myself so I could try out all my equipment and see if I had overlooked anything in my planning. This was ideal because I wouldn't be in the wilderness and there would be park staff working within the park so I would be practicing being alone but not really, if that makes any sense at all. Also, that early in the season there would be few campers around so it would feel as though I were alone.

I packed for that weekend as if I were on my trip. I still hadn't figured out my food and I took some instant rice and pasta meals I found in the grocery store which only required you to add water. I felt these choices were similar to the backpacking meals, but far cheaper. Not much variety and not fully nutritious, but hey, it was only three nights.

I drink tea with milk. As I wouldn't be able to take milk on my trip due to spoiling, I opted instead to drink instant coffee because, oddly enough, the occasional time I drink coffee, I drink it black. Yet I needed to come up with something for my breakfast which was always raw oats with fruit and walnuts. I was happy to remember that a brand of almond milk, which doesn't require refrigeration until opened, comes in drinking boxes - the perfect size to pour on my cereal. As fruit would be too heavy for my trip and this was my practice run, I compromised using raisins, cinnamon and the walnuts, prepackaging each breakfast in an individual baggie. For lunches, I bought crackers, dried salami stick and some hard cheese. I have to say, I was feeling all creative and pretty proud of myself coming up with these meal solutions.

The time for my trial run camping trip arrived and I was excited to be on my way…in the torrential downpour that accompanied me for 1.5 hours, the entire distance from Barrie to Huntsville. It seemed to me to be at its heaviest when I arrived at my campsite.

The site was a large and flat amidst a predominantly coniferous forest and shrubby understory. I sat in my vehicle for a few minutes, wondering if it might ease up, then, reasoning it had been raining hard for the last two hours so why would it stop now, I had my answer. I knew how my tent worked having tried it a few times at home in the yard to refresh my memory, so if I was going to put it up in the rain, at least I wouldn't be standing there trying to figure it out. I should be able to just get to it and get the job done. With all the rain that had fallen, it was easy to see the best spot for the tent where there was no puddle of water collecting. Always appreciate the positives.

It did go fast and it went smooth but still there was a bit of water in the tent that snuck in through the screen before I got the fly in place over top. It didn't take too much to get that wiped up and it wasn't too long after that I had my tent all cozy with my sleeping bag and personal items all set up. I even had an inflatable pillow. Just a small one made specifically for backpacking, but an indulgence indeed, when you consider the plan is a backcountry camping experience. I may as well confess right now, I also bought a low profile, small footprint, inflatable sleeping pad for under my sleeping bag, also made for backpacking. I would like to say that was a necessity, at least more so than the pillow.

Naturally, the rain let up shortly after I was finished getting organized, which was nice, but not being the type of person to let rain get in my way, it was just a bonus for me. Tom, always says the biggest catastrophe is only a minor inconvenience – if you're prepared…and we try to live like that. I was prepared for rain.

It was very quiet in the campground and my site was at the end of a road in the loop to turnaround. There were no other campers within sight of me. It was perfect.

After set up, it was time to go for a hike and I followed the trail through the forest, until it crested a hill and opened up to the view of a smooth, post downpour, steel grey Arrowhead Lake. Making my way through the dripping trees to the shoreline, I followed the lake around to the south shore, my footprints making the first tracks in sand washed clean of any signs made by earlier hikers. It's a small lake, and landlocked, so I hadn't brought my canoe but I had brought my new paddleboard, a gift to myself after turning 65 that January. This lake was ideal for someone with little experience on a paddleboard. There was no risk of being blown out of reach of land and the waves on the lake could only get so big with such a short fetch.

I never came across one person on that hike, most likely due to the recent rain. There was only me and that sound you hear when the wind is playing amongst the trees along with the resultant splatter of drops being shed from moisture laden branches. It is a fine thing to witness nature in its every mood and right now it seemed subdued, slowly rebuilding energy spent from the earlier torrential rains. I believe you see more in inclement weather simply because there are fewer people about so I was constantly scanning about, watching for the unexpected. Meanwhile, ravens moved in from afar, at play, squawking and darting back and forth in the canopy, moving through the forest.

No Expiry

It was dinnertime when I returned to my campsite and I had a little fun with my jump rope while waiting for some water to boil. Unlike in September when I would be in the backcountry and had to purify my water, here in the campground, I did not. There is treated water available at taps throughout and I simply had to walk and fill up a container. In no time at all I was ready to eat my instant "just add water" mac and cheese, but there was a blip. Yes, you simply added water, but what I had missed when reading the instructions in the grocery store was then you were to microwave it. Well…that was a big fail. I allowed it to sit for 15 minutes and while it did soften up the noodles somewhat, it was still crunchy. Not the best meal experience especially with the other problem. The picnic table and everything else on site was soaking wet, so I ate standing up, refusing to sit in my vehicle. That, I decided, would be cheating.

A quick clean up while water boiled for my few dishes and a short time later I was again walking with my travel mug full of herbal tea. Initially I ambled at a relaxed pace on the campground roads but the lure of the trail heading off into the forest toward the lake was too much to resist, so I picked up my pace and veered off with intention.

The wind had died away and along the shoreline as far as I could see, the trees stood still in the evening air as low clouds of mist drifted amongst them, gauzy ghosts floating in unhurried synchronicity.

I was ecstatic when I found a large rock that was dry and so I sat for a good long time; an observer of nature, a being of awareness wrapped in contentment.

Eventually I made my way back to my campsite and decided to go and have a shower at the comfort station. I knew this was to be a practice run as close as possible to my solo wilderness trip where there would be no shower, taps or running water, but I was okay with this especially as I still had no dry place to sit. The unadjustable shower was a hot experience and didn't I come back looking like a lobster!

Again, the rain started and I scurried into my tent with my book and wondered how well I would sleep during the night. I did wake up a few times. One time I woke up to a slight breeze and a cascade of drops that ensued when overhead branches laden with water released their load sounding like the thundering of children's feet heading for the school exit at the sound of the recess bell.

As it turned out, I had a decent sleep. I wasn't lying awake all night in fear, listening for, or imagining, noises in the forest. In fact, I hadn't been afraid at all! This was a good sign! Maybe all that meditation I had been practicing was doing something.

My first morning was a chilly one. First item of business was to get to the lake and do a video on the shoreline for my fitness account @grandma_moves on Instagram. Once that was out of the way, I returned to my tent, got my bathing suit and headed back for a swim. I wasn't a cold plunger, but I had just recently challenged Tom to 100 consecutive days of swimming and there was no way I was going to give up no matter how cold the lake was. I did want to get it out of the way and get that box checked off, though.

As it turned out, the cold air made the lake feel warm by comparison and the water felt like silk gliding over my skin. I had the beach to myself. I had the entire lake to myself. I could almost imagine there was no one else at all in the entire campground.

Things were still wet and I spent a lot of time standing up. Even though the rain had stopped, the picnic table was still wet and would be for a while yet. I went for another hike, this time taking a forest trail and campground roads to Big Bend Lookout, an exposed river delta left over from the Ice Age, and then followed a river trail to Stubb's Falls. The flow of water at the falls was fraught with fury after yesterday's heavy rain. While I was there, the sun came out, making its way through the leaves and landing on the ground in splintered light like paint splatters. In another spot, the sun was just at the perfect angle through an overhead branch to imprint the outlay of its leaves onto a flat rock canvas.

Later that afternoon, a paddleboard session was on tap. It was an amazing experience, both because it was my second time ever out on a board and first time without anyone around. I was glad I had refused my husband's help inflating it the first time I ever used it so I could be confident in doing it now. I drove down to the day-use parking lot where I knew I could find a grassy spot to inflate it with only a short downhill carry to the water. Everything went well and I was feeling pretty pleased with myself as I pushed out into the water and clambered up on the board. The only sound out there was the wind in my ears and the slap of the short, ridged wavelets I was riding over.

I typically wear a hat when I am outdoors, but I didn't wear one on the board because if it blew or fell off, it would be gone, so I left my hair free to blow in the wind. It's short and newly grey after allowing years of colouring to grow out exposing what had been going on underneath. Even though it wasn't very long, it was free to flap around in wild abandon in the nice little breeze that was happening out on the lake. It was liberating and I felt a bit defiant, breaking my self-imposed rule of always wearing a hat in the sun – no matter what. Maybe it was not enough to make me feel quite like a warrior, but perhaps a little like a rule-breaker. It had me grinning.

Out on the horizon, or rather, just out of reach of the horizon, was a line of fluffy summer clouds floating without a care, yet in an orderly fashion without any one cloud trying to overtake the other. I was thinking; if we could only live our lives like that…being together, working as a team, supportive and happy in our role and not trying to take over control of things.

It had been a great day full of activity, and I wasn't finished yet. Back at the campsite, I had another jump rope session which was just as enjoyable as the day before. There was nothing that could beat the sound of a 1/4lb weighted rope whistling as it cut through the air.

I was in bed early again that second night and I woke up the next morning at 6:30am with the realization how well I had slept all night. I had a visitor who woke me up around 3am to the sound of sniffing at my tent right where my head was, then a moment later it was sniffing at the other side of the tent at the door. I clapped my hands and that was the last I heard of it. More than likely it was a raccoon, a common guest in campgrounds. If the sniffing had of been accompanied by a grunting, like a bear, I would have been petrified, but honestly, and even more surprisingly to me, I wasn't even scared. I pondered this. Was I not scared because even though there wasn't anyone nearby, I was still in a campground? Was it because I was older and was maybe less fearful? I decided it was more my determination to do this solo trip and realizing the nights were going to be my biggest hurdle, and I needed to get tough mentally. You know, I barely recognized myself these days. Who was this new gal pushing out of her comfort zone and trying things – hard things! I wanted to get to know her better.

Only minutes after waking, I heard the patter of rain on my tent. I hurried down to the lake in the spotty rain to get my fitness video done and posted, happy to have an umbrella with me to protect my phone from the weather. The rest of the morning was spent hiking in the rain and on one trail I came upon a Ruffed Grouse who came rushing out of the underbrush and planted itself right before me on the trail, blocking my way and putting on quite the performance of lifting its wings and dancing about before disappearing back under the shrubbery.

It was mid afternoon and I had put off going for my swim as the air was much colder than yesterday. It had to be now or I was going to end up having a time convincing myself. The sky looked as though it was trying to break up with little holes of blue interspersed amongst the heavy grey clouds, none of which had yet lined up with the sun. Getting in the water was easy. I just didn't think about it and marched right in. While I was in the water, the sun did come out a few times, and it felt amazing. I was certain it was going to come out and stay out at any moment as the clouds seemed to be spreading apart more and I sat on shore with a towel wrapped around me, shivering a bit, waiting. When it did come out, as nice as it was, it wasn't enough against the coolness of the wind. I headed back to my campsite, changed and warmed up with a jump rope session.

At the exact time I was heating my dinner, it began to rain again so I quickly packed everything away and sat in my tent to eat and then read for the rest of the evening.

Before I knew it, it was my last day. It had rained off and on throughout the night, at times a downpour. It was another rainy and cold morning so I set off to get my daily video done at the beach, came back and ate breakfast in the tent. There was no letting up in the weather and I was tired of standing up all the time with nowhere dry to sit unless I was in my tent, so I packed up my wet abode and was on my way home by mid-morning. I had planned to do another hike before leaving, but I was okay with not getting that done. The trip had served its purpose. It was successful and my very first solo camping experience was wonderful, even if it was in a public campground.

From this trip, I learned the following: 1) Almond milk is too heavy for my backcountry trip so I need to use powdered milk instead. 2) Bring a tarp. 3) Add something in addition to my sleeping bag to stay warm. 4) Bring a deck of cards in case I am stuck in my tent for a long time. 5) Definitely find a chair that is lightweight for backpacking so I can sit down.

DECISIONS, DECISIONS

Tell me, what is it you plan to do with your one wild and precious life ~ Mary Oliver

When I got home from my trial run of camping on my own, I was anxious to acquire everything I needed for my September trip. I wanted to practice packing everything in my backpack, weigh it and learn the best order of placing things inside. True, it was only early June, but we had lots of camping trips with the trailer planned and I would be away for long stretches. If I wanted to be organized, and I was going to be, I needed to move on this.

I went to the outfitters looking for quality dried food to make sure my trip was going to be the most pleasurable experience possible. I spent a lot of time scanning the wall of dried food. From floor to ceiling there were several rows of different brands and countless options. There were vegan and vegetarian meals, meals which sounded anything but something you'd eat on a camping trip in the middle of nowhere - such as Jambalaya, Sweet and Sour Pork and Quinoa with Veggies and Tahini Sauce, as well as comfort foods like Lasagna and Shepherd's Pie. How does one begin to make a decision?

I was looking for single serve packages but everything seemed to be two servings. I hadn't considered this problem. After some thought, I decided that would work out fine. I would hydrate a pack at lunch, eat half and seal the rest up to eat for dinner, thus consuming the whole package and no extra food to deal with.

Problem solved. I bought enough to last 5 nights instead of three. Always, always take extra.

Next thing to deal with was water purification. I stood in the aisle in front of a display of endless options available to make sure my lake water was going to be potable. Problem was, I didn't know where to begin even though I had researched this and knew what I wanted. None of the brands I listed as possibilities were before me. Now I wasn't so sure. Were some of these options better than what I had found online? Were they newer, more reliable methods? There was a store employee just in the next aisle patiently assisting a customer and giving the pros and cons of each backpacking cookstove under consideration. He sounded very knowledgeable and so I waited for him to finish up.

Eventually he came to me and I explained what I was planning on doing and that I wanted to know what was the best way to ensure safe drinking water out there. It quickly became apparent as he simply pointed out an item with no dialogue whatsoever, that he was not interested in me. A 65 year old woman with grey hair does not spell adventure and excitement. I became invisible to him. Again, I felt the closed door that is ageism. Proving that I wasn't imagining things, he quickly moved on to a father and young son who moved in alongside me also eyeing the water purification display. The employee spent more time with them when the father already knew what he wanted, had located it easily and was standing there with package in hand. I overheard him say they were going on a canoe trip.

The employee moved off and the father and son remained, so I decided to ask the dad what he used to purify water on his trips. This man was so helpful, I couldn't have asked for better. He told me what he uses, and why. He also told me it was prudent to use two treatments as he knew of someone who got very sick even though they used a popular treatment and ever since, he has used two. That made very good sense to me. I couldn't even imagine what it would be like to be out in the wilderness sick and weak and having to paddle lakes and carry a canoe and backpack great distances through the forest.

I gratefully thanked the man and his son, wished them well on their upcoming trip and selected the two treatments he recommended.

There were other items I intended to purchase that day but I was put off at the lack of help I received from the employee, so I decided to leave those items for another day.

If you desire to go into the wilderness and experience all the peace and wonderment nature can provide, there is no getting around the fact there are bears. That is just how it is. The question was, how was I going to deal with this and make certain bears weren't going to be dining on my food?

I had studied several different methods of securing your food bag up in a tree several hundred feet away from your campsite, but when I practiced at home in my own forest, it hadn't been going well. Simply toss the rope over a branch at least 15 feet high from the ground and at least 3 feet away from the trunk of the tree. First off, in a dense forest there are so many branches around and interlocking there was not a way to do that without getting snarled in other branches. The internet always has solutions, and it said to attach a stone or weighted item to the end of the rope to carry it through the air and over the branch. I had an unsettling vision of it sailing up, over the selected branch, if I were lucky, and then with the momentum, spinning around and around the branch securing that rope there forever with no means of getting it free and standing there with the food bag in one hand and the now useless rope end in the other with no options remaining for making my food secure.

Another school of thought used two trees that were spaced at least 10 feet apart and, using ropes, hoisting the food bag up in the middle. All well and good if you found trees set apart perfectly like goal posts in a soccer pitch. I was getting anxious about this food bag safety thing. I dreamed about it. I walked around our forest constantly looking up at the trees and wondering how I would get the bag up in that tree, or maybe that one over there. I was not confident.

The research continued.

I allowed myself to let go of the tried and true "old way" of dealing with food in the wilderness and broadened my search. I found that bear proof canisters are mandatory in some U.S. National Parks depending on types of bears (black bears or grizzlies) and how dense their population is. In fact, in some of these parks where bears are numerous, and hungry, food bags are not allowed and you can be fined if you don't use a bear canister. The very best part was bear canisters don't hang in a tree. They can be placed on the ground a good distance from your campsite.

Not only did this tell me all I needed to know, it was exactly what I wanted to hear to have the confidence to move away from the need to use the longstanding tradition of the food bag hung in a tree. This was such a huge relief. I felt giddy. Tossing aside the food bag meant not worrying if it poured rain and made it wet or if raccoons got into it – after all, they can climb out branches quite easily, or, a more likely scenario, not being able to locate the perfect tree with the right sized branch at the right height and then ending up compromising with the bag being hung too low or on an unsafe branch barely able to support the weight of it. I had been agonizing over this for months and here was a simple solution.

A few days later I was at a large outfitters and purchased my bear canister. The one I selected was approved by the U.S. National Park Service for use against all types of bears. I reasoned if it was effective against grizzly bears then most certainly it could handle the smaller black bears we have in Ontario.

The canister is a bright yellow with a highly reflective band around it which makes it so easy to find in the dark. It seals tight with a keyed system of three locks, and while this sounds complicated and might instill instant fear of losing a key while out there, it wasn't a worry. Anything at all can act as a key. A coin will do it, or any metal item resembling a slotted tip screwdriver. I got very high tech and fancy, slipping a shoelace through a rectangular piece of metal Tom found for me and placing it around my neck. This lock method meant it took a little time to get into the bear canister compared to some of the other ones available, but it was also what made it more secure. This thing was going to keep my food and toiletries away from bears, and, ultimately, that was all that mattered to me. The compromise was, it was a heavy beast in the bottom of my backpack, weighing in at close to 2 kg. I was happy to add this weight to my pack for the peace of mind it would allow.

What is it about a bear canister that keeps bears out of your food when you simply set it on the ground out in the open, a few hundred yards away from your campsite? It is made from very strong material. Mine is a polymer blend. The canisters are smooth with no edges for a bear to get its teeth on to pry it open. Also, bears don't have opposing thumbs so they aren't going to pick up your canister and walk away with it while whistling a tune.

Aside from being a very effective method of protecting your food, it also means safety for the bear. Once a bear becomes familiar with the idea they can easily obtain food from humans and they have had success, the animal is going to end up being put down because now it is a risk to all humans it may encounter. When we think of going into the wilderness and "leaving no trace", aside from not leaving garbage behind, it also means not impacting nature's balance in any way. Indeed, it is a fact Algonquin Park has had to kill between 50 and 100 bears some years which become nuisance bears because people have not put their food away properly. Not only tragic, but unnecessary.

While I was thinking about bears, I stopped by the sporting section and picked up a can of bear spray. There were two sizes of the spray and the gentleman behind the counter asked me which I preferred. I smiled and said as I wasn't planning to meet any bears at all, I would just take the small can. I felt prepared and confident as I left the store with my bear canister and bear spray, that is until I got home and read the bear spray can to familiarize myself with the product. The entire can empties in 7 seconds. Maybe I should have opted for the large…

The following week the topographic map I had ordered of the area I would be tripping in arrived in the mail. This may sound weird, but I couldn't wait to open it and lay my eyes on it. There is nothing better than looking at a map and studying the contour lines, imagining hills and valleys and looking at lakes with inlets and bays knowing I would be paddling in that very spot. To me, it was almost like reading a story. While I already had a map (five, actually) of Algonquin Park which clearly showed the canoe routes, a topographic map was much more detailed, was a larger scale and also recommended.

All that was left to get was a chair. I had no idea what it would look like carrying a chair into the wilderness, portaging from lake to lake, but I knew I wanted one after my wet weekend trial run in the campground when I did a lot of standing around.

I ventured back to the outfitters where I had experienced the smack of ageism full on. I knew what I wanted after researching and learning what was available so my strategy was just to go in and pick out my chair and leave. I didn't need to rely on assistance.

I came out of there with the coolest chair I've ever seen! Bright and vibrant colours, lightweight as anything I could have imagined, yet strong! Easy to put together and take apart and so small and compact – it was worth the ridiculous price I paid for it. I was in love…with a chair! I rushed home and assembled it outside, posting the process on Instagram to allow everyone to see how cool this grandma was with a tie dye chair.

Now I had everything I would need and with the same excitement you experience getting ready to go to your first ever concert, I spread it all across the porch and proceeded to pack my backpack again and again to find the best order of things.

It occurred to me that it is actually easier when there are at least two people tripping together because you can evenly distribute the load of all the things you only need one of, like the cookstove, bear canister, tent and pots etc. However, this was not an option to consider. It was my trip and I was going it alone.

IT KIND OF FEELS LIKE HOME

There is a way that nature speaks, that land speaks. Most of the time we are simply not patient enough, quiet enough, to pay attention to the story ~ Linda Hogan

Algonquin Provincial Park is the oldest provincial park in Canada, having been established in 1893. It is 7,653 square kilometres, has over 2400 lakes and over 1,200 kilometres of streams and rivers. Algonquin, in other words, is massive. To have this park, a land of wild animals in their natural habitat and endless waterways threading through wilderness of pristine beauty, means a lot to Ontarians. It is a bucket list destination for outdoor types worldwide.

People flock to the ribbon of highway through the south end of the park known as Hwy 60 in April when it is probable to see a moose roadside enjoying the remnant winter road salt. It's an impressive beast to see. People continue to come all summer long to camp, hike, paddle and enjoy the environment that comes with a park this size. In October, when the air cools, Ontario forests are alive with vibrant coloured leaves and people amass to the area with their cameras, snaking up the highway for hours in muddled traffic for a few hours of peaceful joy and walks in soft sunshine along the lakes or on the trails. There are no swimmers this time of year.

Kiosk Campground, in the north part of the park, is not very well known as compared to the more popular and larger campgrounds located along the much busier Hwy 60 corridor in the south part of the park. Kiosk is an out of the way, small campground of just 29 campsites, many of them on the shore of the lake, and it exists as a jump off access point to numerous canoe routes. Kiosk offers little in terms of amenities, lots in terms of backcountry paddling opportunity. There are no electrical sites, no showers, no cell service, one flush toilet and four compost toilets, which tends to make it less desirable to campers used to the convenience of daily showers and regular washrooms.

To arrive, you follow a 30 km road which strikes off on its own, leaving behind the Trans-Canada Highway and clinging to the Amable du Fond River, to wind through forest, rock, meadow, farmland and the hamlet of Eau Claire until you reach the northwest corner of Algonquin Park at Kioshkokwi Lake.

Kioshkokwi is the Algonquin name for the lake and translates to Lake of Gulls. When I stand at water's edge and let my eye follow the shoreline, I conjure up images of the past when indigenous people traveled here. Would they recognize it, those people of the past? The forest still hugs the lake, which still reflects the sky where the trees still whisper to each other. I believe they would.

Carmen Cross has been managing the Kiosk Campground since 1997 and I met her in 2016, the first year we pulled our trailer up there. Every year since, when we arrive the first place I go is to the office to say hello. I go over for a chat every few days when I see she isn't with customers and each time I do, I came back with more knowledge. Not just about the campground and the many stories Carmen has from her long tenure here as manager, but about trees, lakes, animals and birds. We rhyme off books we've read related to the natural world, adding to our already long lists of "want to read". There is no stopping two book people when they get together.

No Expiry

Carmen doesn't just work here, she actually lives in the back part of the office from April to October. How did this woman end up with the job of managing a campground for over 26 years, living on site all season year after year? The first thing she will tell you is this isn't a job. It's a lifestyle.

Years earlier, she was a mom of four children working at a department store, which she enjoyed, but she knew she was capable of more. She decided to return to school and in her 40's, Carmen found herself attending Nipissing University for Environmental Science – Physical Geography. During her final year she happened to see a tender opportunity in a local newspaper to operate the Kiosk Campground at Algonquin Park. Application submitted, she forgot all about it until the following February when she was notified she had been awarded the tender. That is when everything changed.

This job of managing the campground is busy. It is physically demanding, long hours and it is everything Carmen could have ever hoped for. It has made her see the importance of having a place like this for people to come to, immerse themselves in the surroundings and take something home with them, something which makes them return again and again to seek peace.

"We take for granted that we can go on a trail and find peace", she says, noting that recent visitors from the Netherlands told her they had to line up to go for a nature walk on a trail at home. Here, people can just come and participate in nature at their leisure. It is here for them whenever they are ready. Carmen has made it her responsibility to make peoples' experience special and memorable. Her personal mission statement is that in the capacity of being in charge of the campground, to look after it the best way she knows how, providing the best experience for visitors.

All these years later, she is still helping others discover what nature has for them.

With all the memories from decades of caring for Kiosk that feed her soul, connecting her to the natural world, Carmen hopes to have the same enthusiasm for life when she is done here and to be able to take her camera and binoculars and have that awe, that energy, to follow a bird through the forest. I don't see anything stopping her.

I feel this place. It fits like a favourite pair of jeans. I know the peace Carmen speaks of. I have always understood nature on its terms. Until age five, I lived tucked away in the heart of nature, not too far from Kiosk campground, as coincidence would have it. Surrounded by water, trees, animals, birds and reptiles. I had no knowledge of a larger, outside world.

I had a vivid and active imagination as a young child. Not surprising when one has no idea there was anyone other than adults in the world. Nature was my playground and I visited my favourite trees daily, talked to butterflies and watched bugs with curiosity. This was my foundation and I have always had it with me regardless where life found me at any given time.

My parents divorced when I was just nine months old and I was sent to live with my grandparents and great-grandparents at a hunting/fishing lodge they owned and operated on the outskirts of Mattawa. Located deep in the forest where the trees met the shores of Lake Champlain, it was my home. My mother stayed in Toronto on her own, continuing at her job.

I grew up there, at the lodge, not knowing I had anyone else outside of these four humans, then three when my great-grandfather passed away, who loved and nurtured me through my formative years. Of course, they were busy running a business – leading guided trips, making meals, cleaning rooms… and the day was mine to explore and let my imagination entertain me. I was very good at both.

The hunting dogs were my friends. When they weren't out with the hunters eager to find deer, they were my playmates. They all had their names, but I gave them different names. They were secret friends.

There were snapping turtles to observe, once right at the water's edge where my bare toes stood resolutely mere inches from the laser like stare of one eyeing them up as tasty morsels, the sunlight through the shallows playing ripples on my foot as if there was no danger whatsoever. For whatever reason, I backed away, luckily unscathed. Where were my grandparents at the time? In the lodge, working away, thinking I was upstairs in my bedroom having my afternoon nap. I was a bit of a rascal.

Dinnertime was a busy time at the lodge, with all the guests needing to be fed. I always ate alone but it was the best time. I had a small table and chairs just my size set up right in front of an old black and white television and each night I ate while Bugs Bunny and the Road Runner amused me with their silly antics. Sometimes I wore a head band while I ate that my grandfather made of corrugated cardboard with partridge feathers stuck in it after a successful bird hunt by the hunters.

I remember summer bedtimes when my window was open wide and I would go to sleep to the gurr-rump of frogs and sometimes the call of the whip-poor-will. I only remember happy times there, as it should be for a child, and I will always be grateful I had those stable years as a solid base before being uprooted and moved to Toronto to live with my mother and her new husband so I could begin Kindergarten. This was a culture shock move. From deep forest filled with birdsong and wolf cries to concrete and asphalt punctuated with blaring horns and sirens. Instead of trees there were tall buildings that poked into the sky and hid the sun at sunrise and sunset. From loving grandparents to two people I did not know and who did not know me. It was difficult. Yet I always had that love and curiosity for nature in my back pocket and I would find it in the middle of a dandelion flower or the underside of a leaf. There was still nature to be found, however microscopic it was. This is what grounded me going forward into what turned into 15 tumultuous and challenging years.

I still have a reverence for the natural world and it draws me to it unapologetically – and I follow. There is marvel at the spider weaving its intricate web, joy at birdsong filling the air, solace in the forest, promise in the sunrise and peace in the endless starry sky at night. It isn't just mine. It belongs to all of us.

It doesn't take long to understand my desire to do this trip alone. I had been alone in nature at the beginning of my life since I first learned to walk and it was time to reconnect. I think of it as similar to having a best friend and seeing them all the time but never being alone with them to talk. We were about to have some quality time together, just like the old days.

AND I'M OFF!

There are some places in life where you can only go alone. Embrace the beauty of your solo journey ~ Mandy Hale

Nervous? Nope. Unsure? Nope. How about exhilarated? Yes! That would be the feeling I had the morning of departure. Here it was, the day I had dreamed of for years but I kept coming up with excuses and telling myself I wasn't capable. I had ample help from society telling me I wouldn't be able to manage on my own, particularly being a woman my age. Mentally, I had worked hard these past months to prepare so this solo trip would go as smoothly as possible. Today I would launch myself into the unknown to be swallowed up by green forests, blue lakes and all the wild things that lived there and experience nature totally on my own. It really wasn't an odd thing to do when you stopped to consider that we humans are nature, too. We are part of this.

I purposely took the morning slow, walking Cedar on our usual route; out of the campground and down a gravel lane cutting through towering pines, stones crunching underfoot, to where a bridge of honey coloured lumber, not yet turned grey by the seasons, spanned the river. It was here we would often see a Great Blue Heron hopeful for breakfast, head tilted with laser focus on the frothy whitewater swirling around its feet, spilling over and around the large, flat rock it stood on. As expected, it was there, in its favourite spot. Two Mergansers allowed themselves to be pulled into the downstream V of the fast moving water and bobbed along doing nothing at all to steer themselves, turning sideways and then straight, always synchronized, as they dropped from level to level in the rapids looking very much like plastic ducks in a race at a community picnic. The heron lifted off soundlessly and headed downstream in surprising elegance despite its long legs and large wingspan, settling at the next bend in the river.

I took all of it in: my surroundings, the smells, the sounds and the feeling of total relaxation and the joy of being in this space.

A short time later I was back at the trailer sitting having a tea with Tom, taking in these moments in awareness with a calmness that surprised me. Typically I would be wound up with excitement and eager to get started on a new adventure. Another unexpected side of myself I didn't know existed. Tom and I ate breakfast together, Cedar sleeping, snoring softly with his heavy head lying across my foot so he would be alerted should I get up. Did he know something was up? I wondered if he would miss me.

It had rained during the night and I had listened to it, but didn't fret because it's simply weather and as long as you have the proper clothing to keep dry you have nothing to worry about. Rain to me is meditative and I have been known to go for walks or even run in it. There is nothing like listening to the patter on leaves to quiet the soul. The humidity was high and it was warm for so early in the morning. Ideal conditions for the showers and thunderstorms they were calling for later on this day.

Finally, it was time. I felt a surge of energy and a readiness for the journey to start. I was confident the physical part of paddling, carrying my canoe, backpacks and tent over rough terrain wasn't going to be an issue. I have worked out consistently since 1980. It was going to be the mental aspect, but I had been working on that, too. The fact I was going at all was proof I had overcome those mental barriers. Still, there were the nights to contend with. We would see how well I did. Some nights when I had lain awake thinking about this trip, I wondered how I was going to manage out in the wilderness when it got dark and I couldn't simply say "I'm done...", and walk back to civilization and safety. This was the heaviest thing on my mind.

It was 8:30am when I pushed off into the lake, my gear secured in the canoe, Tom and Cedar watching from shore. One of them was a little anxious for me, the other one wondered who was going to feed him. You would probably be right no matter who you chose there.

Right away I was getting wet, soaked actually, because being used to a canoe paddle I had no idea how to use a double ended paddle and I was pretty sure I was doing it wrong as I don't believe it was intended to scoop so much water out of the lake with each stroke. My pants quickly became sodden and lay plastered against my legs from my hips down. This little issue, an immediate problem that needed to be overcome, made me forget to turn around and wave goodbye to my boys before disappearing around a point and out of their line of sight.

Kioshkokwi Lake is a large lake that can get quite choppy and angry with a west wind coming down the length of it, as it so often does, but on this morning it was a calm and lazy pussycat. I moved effortlessly through the water, scanning the shoreline and easily picking out a white pine towering above all the other trees on the horizon. Whenever you see a tree sticking out way above the others, chances are good it's a white pine. The sky was reflected in the water and the birds that I saw heading west last night to their roosting spot were now flying easterly on their morning commute to find food. There is a rhythm to everything.

There is an abandoned railway with the tracks taken up leaving behind only the heavy slag as a nod to a past time when the iron horses traveled through these lands, connecting isolated communities and carrying lumber from the mills. It snakes east along the north side of the lake, crossing at a narrow section where a trestle links the two shores before the railway is off again, galloping into the forest to the next lake and it is when I am carried by the current through this narrow passage underneath this trestle that I feel the journey has really begun. I think of it as a gateway where I leave the old me behind - the one who almost let society dictate what I was able to do now that I was of a certain age. I was happy to leave that gal behind, as well as that society.

I reached into my pack for my phone, taking it out of its waterproof bag to take a video all while I maneuvered to keep straight through some rocks and pass underneath the trestle. I was certain this was going to be an epic video looking up as I crossed to the other side. As it turned out, it wasn't. It didn't look like anything at all, just grey clouds and suddenly some boards with glimpses of sky in between, yet it was a record of that moment.

A peacefulness embraced me. It'd been there since I first dipped the paddle into the lake. This was my dream and it was really happening. I made it happen. We always hear of people realizing their dreams, striving for them and making them happen and now I fully understood why it is important to work towards them. I felt every cell of my being. I felt alive. It had been so easy to just dream and not take action, keeping my desire tethered to me yet not allowing it access to being a part of my life. I did that because it was safe. I couldn't fail if I didn't do it. I couldn't feel fully alive, either. I realized this now. How many years had I come up with excuses not to have to do this yet at the same time wanting it so badly, feeling torn between the two? Imagine not experiencing this moment with the excitement that was coursing through my veins! This had always been a goal that I was fully capable of, yet fear anchored me to the shore watching and wanting. I was feeling grateful right at that moment.

Watching a line of orderly ducks fly overhead, I stopped paddling and drifted in the stillness listening to the air whistle through their feathers with each beat of their wings. I found myself thinking, I was one with all. This trip was going to be amazing.

I changed direction from east to south, heading for the marsh. I know the portage I'm looking for is deep within this marshy area and as I approach it, I slow down and scan the shoreline hoping to see the Bald Eagle hunting that Tom and I saw here last year when we paddled around the lake, but if it still frequents here, it was feeding elsewhere on this morning.

There is a well defined channel through the marsh from season after season of trippers moving through yet I quickly see there are some very shallow spots to it where I think my canoe might get hung up. Each stroke I take hits bottom and I ease the canoe over to where it looks a little deeper in order to get around some submerged deadwood that had drifted and become mired in the grasses until the marsh bottom claimed it as its own, covering it each season with dead organic matter that slowly builds. The evolution of things.

Then I am there. Nice flat, sandy shoreline appears through the towering grasses and awaits me and my canoe. It's obvious this is part of a popular canoe route with the sand scarred from the keels of canoes that have been pulled from the water by other paddlers who began their journeys in the days and weeks before me. The sand rubs against the bottom of my canoe as I ride up softly onto the shore. It's the first portage of my trip. I feel like the boss. I climb out of my canoe and briefly consider my drenched pants before deciding not to worry about it.

There is the slightest ripple of water flowing by from a small river which thins, then spreads wide over a delta cutting narrow vein-like streamlets that empty into the lake. It's a soft rushing, soothing and steady, keeping equilibrium. I admire it for a few minutes, the water skipping, falling over itself, playful in its journey and then turn to my canoe, hands on hips, to figure out my strategy for carrying.

I have a large backpack, a small backpack, heavy tent in a carry case, my paddle and lifejacket as well as the canoe. It is a given that it has to be two trips, which means traversing every portage three times in total, but I want to make it as

Sheila Nollert

*First portage
Kioshkokwi to Little Mink*

efficient as possible. I decide to take the canoe over first, wearing my small backpack at the same time, and leave my large backpack and tent for the second trip.

If one thing seems to hold true in this world, it is that if any other canoeists come along and see a canoe sitting on the shore or a backpack, it won't be touched. Apparently, no one remembers any such time when someone had something stolen…by a person, at least. It has been the occasion, though, when a bear has snatched a backpack left on the trail if there is food in it.

I decided not to tempt fate and risk such a devastating turn of events as losing my stuff to theft my first day out and conceal my backpack and tent in the forest, well off the trail. I clipped my lifejacket to a thwart, jammed the paddle alongside the seat of the canoe so it wouldn't fall out, put on my small backpack and hoisted the canoe over my head. I was off.

Let's be clear, not every portage is a lovely woodland footpath padded with a layer of red pine needles like you might find in an urban area. Rocks shaped like triangular teeth jutting from the ground remind me of sharks and threaten me on this portage to Little Mink Lake. I simply march around, ignoring them while being mindful at the same time. Gnarled, arthritic looking fingers of tree roots reach for me, too. Some have scuff marks across them indicating a confrontation with someone earlier who wasn't watching where they stepped. There are spots the stones crunch loudly beneath each step and in other areas I can't be heard, the sound muffled out by decaying, wet leaf litter underfoot. Being it is the very first portage of my trip, I have no idea how long it will take me to get to the next lake other than I know the distance is 635 metres.

I climb up a rise through the trees where the trail levels out, curling around a murky swamp draped with twisted, woody vines and tattered mosses where there was nothing but dead quiet to greet me. I try to keep my eye on it as I pass, even though my vision is limited due to the canoe over my head, because it looks like something mean and nasty could be very happy living in there. Everything wore a coat of a vibrant, slimy green and reeked of decay.

I got by the swamp and found the forest thickened with cedars. I smell their aromatic scent before I see them for what they are. There is no mistaking the woodsy smell reminiscent of pencil shavings and antique hope chests.

I can hear rapids not yet in sight, at least not from under the canoe, running alongside the portage. It is the same river that empties so tamely by the time it reaches the start of the portage at Kioshkokwi Lake. It is heavily shaded here, and cool, with the noise of the rapids loud enough to drown out any other sounds. I considered that if I couldn't hear an animal, then an animal couldn't hear me, so I begin to sing. The Lion Sleeps Tonight…maybe not the best song selection when in the forest where wild animals may be lurking. I was off key and I forgot the words so I just made them up. Any animal would run the other way.

I kept going and eventually came to where the railway dissects the trail and now descends down, still following the river, into an even darker, thicker part of the forest. Chickadees darted in front of me from one side of the trail to the other. They are close enough I can hear them more than catch glimpses of them from the underside of my canoe. I felt good and was having no problem carrying the canoe but I couldn't help wondering how much further it was. Then, in the distance, the shades of greens, greys and browns are broken with blue. There is nothing like finally glimpsing the next lake through the trees. My destination.

It is tricky footwork getting down to water's edge . Slowly working my way down, at times sidestepping, I am happy to finally set the canoe down on the shore at the bottom of a very steep embankment. I rubbed the back of my neck. This wasn't unexpected. I had read on a trip report online that some trippers actually do a longer portage using the abandoned railway to bypass this steep entry into Little Mink Lake which does two things. One, you have an easy, level entry into Mink Lake avoiding the steep embankment into Little Mink Lake, and two,

Little Mink is so small, it resembles a puddle jump to the next portage that takes you to the larger Mink Lake. It's a quick load your canoe, short paddle, unload, portage that can be avoided if you bypass the small lake altogether.

Anyone who knows me could have won a wager that I wouldn't have chosen to bypass this little lake just to make things easier. I chose to do it as it is laid out on the canoe route map. I am a traditionalist to the best of my abilities.

I headed back to get "The Beast", the name I have already given my 75 litre backpack and 4.5 kg tent. I think of it as a term of endearment, but still, it is refreshingly lovely to hike back empty handed, walking alongside the rapids, past the eerie swamp and even stopping to watch chubby little Black Capped Chickadees bobbing from tree to tree as the flock moved across the portage. Perhaps they were following me, making sure I was safe.

Eventually I am back and my gear is secured in the canoe. Without ceremony I push off shore and head out into Little Mink Lake. I am pleased that I already have a routine in place of what order I am carrying things and how to secure my paddle to the canoe. I also noticed that my pants were almost dry from the walking and only marginally wet from the knees down. The focus now had to be how to paddle without bringing the lake onto my lap. It wasn't long and, out of necessity, I was having much better success with staying dry. Another feel good win! Lesson learned: No need to dig the paddle deep into the water and pull out buckets of water that rush down the handle onto your lap. Keep the paddle chest height, close, and just simply dip each blade into the water. Works perfectly.

Little Mink is like a hidden, untouched gem. The pines crowd the shoreline and in some places overhang the lake possessively as if trying to keep it a secret from the world. The size of the lake means it is still and reflective, having no waves. A small, but picturesque tree-clad rock face rose up from the black depths along the shore on my right as I paddled out, its mirror image perfectly reflected in the motionless lake. Gently, I turned the canoe to face it head on so I could really see it and know it a little better instead of just passing by. It doesn't look accessible with a few tall, straight pines running along in front of it almost like a fence and a heavy cloak of lichen on the rocks. I was fascinated by the lichen, knowing it grows slowly at approximately 5 – 8mm a year, with the realization these large patches are likely hundreds of years old.

A small mound of bright green new growth on a submerged log was distracting in its vibrant dressing while lily pads floated in scattered array nearby, the only things breaking the reflections of the shoreline.

I checked my watch to find it's just after 11am when I leave Little Mink Lake behind and set out on the 450 metre portage to the much larger Mink Lake. I find part of the trail laid thick with bright yellow leaves; the season's early departers from the surrounding trees. The portage is uneventful and soon I find myself at Mink Lake. This spot is not too bad for putting into the lake but there are many good sized rocks to dance around to get to the water. This is another first. I can honestly attest I have never danced around large rocks in hiking boots carrying a canoe over my head while wearing a backpack. I am grateful for having the sense to wear my hiking boots. I set down the canoe next to the water and headed back for my gear.

While walking the trail back to Little Mink, I feel a few warning drops of moisture followed by the soft patter of rain. I made a mental note of what I just learned: When it is threatening rain, place your canoe upside-down with the small backpack underneath when you go back for your second carry. I rejoiced a little when it didn't amount to anything and the patter of rain stopped as quickly as it started. The seat in the canoe and my backpack would both still be dry when I got back to them.

This portage is interesting in that part way in there is a fork, looking a little like an off ramp, which leads to another lake and, for some reason or other, it seems funny to me to encounter an intersection out here in the backcountry. It feels urban. I will be using that other trail in a few days when I return as this is the point it will bring me full loop. I look down its length as far as I can see and envision myself with canoe overhead having just finished my third night out in the back country, heading back to the world I left behind and I find myself wondering if I will still feel the same way as I do now and what experiences I will have had by then.

Just before lunch I am ready to push off into Mink Lake. I'm hungry and thirsty, and I had planned to eat lunch each day, but the last thing I want to do right now is unpack my stuff to get to my food and spend 30 minutes purifying water. I am staying overnight on this lake so I decide to push on, find where I want to spend the night and get set up. I will enjoy a late lunch/ early dinner at the spot I will call home for the night.

Mink Lake is long and narrow, about 6 km in length. Paddling happily down the middle, my pants finally dry, I am taking my time and being fully aware of the fact I am right where I want to be at this moment. You cannot beat this feeling.

My eye takes in the far end of the lake and it looks kind of hazy and I briefly wonder if it is raining down there but the thought is gone as quickly as it appears, at least until the first few drops of rain come down and before you know it, I'm paddling in a quiet shower. The lake becomes pock marked for a few minutes until it passes and luckily it wasn't enough to soak me or my gear. My backpack is waterproofed but my daypack is not and even though my phone is in a sealed bag, it is nice that the bag won't be wet against my back when I carry it. My maps are safely in plastic and attached to a thwart in front of me for easy viewing.

The canoe route map shows a campsite past the halfway point of the lake and this is where I head after deciding it would be preferable to have a few kilometres of paddling in the morning to get to the portage rather than camping closer, packing up and pushing off only to have to dismantle a short distance later for

Sheila Nollert

A rocky launch into Mink Lake

the carry to the next lake. This is my strategy in place for tomorrow's portage to Club Lake. It's going to be a long one at 985 metres.

The site I want is vacant, which isn't surprising at all given I haven't seen anyone on the lake other than a glimpse of someone earlier today on a distant shoreline when I first started out. It's mid-September, a quieter time for tripping compared to the warmer summer months when it is conceivable there would be several camping on this lake each night. I am pretty sure I am the only one on the the lake.

I have this desire to call out, "honey, I'm home!" when I step out of my canoe onto the space I am claiming as mine for the night, but I don't. I just smile at the thought. There is a bit of pressure to get set up quickly because as much as I was trying to ignore it, darker clouds are closing in. I am happy with my pace when I am completely set up just 45 minutes later. Inside the tent looks cozy with sleeping bag on top of mat and inflated pillow just waiting for my head. The fist sized battery lantern which activates when the lid is extended and can of bear spray are set within easy reach of my sleeping spot. Pen and journal lay next to my backpack inviting me to do an entry. Next in priority is the task of finding the "thunder box" so I know where it is when I need it. This is a wooden box back from the site within the forest that has a hinged lid which when opened exposes what I would describe as an outhouse without privacy. No walls. You're sitting on a box. You really are in nature in every respect. It matters not as there is no one around to see you sitting there, save for any wild animals thinking what odd creatures we are that we need to use a box.

If you have ever been camping out on crown land in areas which are popular and attract lots of people you would appreciate the "thunder box" or "vault", because it is very disheartening to walk into a meadow that is covered with lumps of tissue as far as the eye can see from a full season of people passing through who didn't know how to deal with their waste properly. It's not only disheartening and an eyesore, but also unhealthy. Most experienced trippers and backpackers know the proper way is to dig a small hole for your waste. Many outdoor people carry a garden hand trough with them for this purpose. Often times it is hanging from their pack.

The vault located, I have everything I need and I head back further into the trees to put my food canister safely back from my campsite. Setting it on the ground about 150 metres away is recommended. I do 200 metres.

As if I feel the need to justify my decision for the bear canister over food bag and rope, I take time to notice everywhere I look the trees are nestled so close there is no hope of throwing a rope up through the interlocking branches. Over the months leading up to the trip I had accumulated a respectable pile of pencil drawings showing the various ways of securing food in a tree after scouring the internet. Every few weeks I would review my findings, laying the scraps of paper out on top of my bed in an orderly fashion as if I were about to engage in a game of strategy, and try to decide which method to use, never arriving at a solution, until I learned of the bear canister. The bear canister was one of my most prized possessions and I had just confirmed, a good decision.

One thing I wanted to do on this trip was jump rope on every lake. Well, who else has ever jumped rope in the wilds of Algonquin Park? I'm willing to bet the answer is no one. I'd been jumping rope for about a year, learning some tricks and becoming thoroughly addicted to the activity and with a rope taking so little room in my pack and negligible added weight, it was coming with me. The other thing I thought would be nice to do is swim on every lake I camped on. It is really easy to decide something like swimming in every lake when you consider it during the hottest part of summer and the water is the temperature of bath water. The lakes in northern Ontario lose their heat quickly once the days become shorter and the nights become cooler, usually by the middle of August, but that wasn't going to stop me once I had made the decision.

*View from my tent
Mink Lake*

First up was jump rope. I had jumped at Little Mink Lake, just briefly. It hadn't been easy to find a suitable spot, but I got it done amongst the rocks and steep shoreline. It wasn't long here until I found a level spot free of grass and roots and jumped in my moccasins. I chose to bring moccasins to wear once I was on my campsite each day and done paddling so I could feel a connection to the earth. That connection wasn't going to happen with ankle high, stiff hiking boots. It felt luxurious to walk around in the pliable leather footwear.

Next was the swim to fully experience this space that was my temporary home. The lake bottom was a little mushy with a shallow entry, not too rocky. The water was nice for swimming and was warmer than I expected as I glided out from shore to tread water for a few minutes while looking up in admiration at my tent before coming back in.

Space in my backpack was at a premium and I had only brought a small hand towel figuring I would mostly air dry after each swim. I didn't dry off as quickly as I had hoped and because I was hungry, I just used the towel. It was quickly heavy with the moisture and I hung it up to dry but it was already late in the day and still threatening rain. It wasn't going to dry.

A few weeks prior to the commencement of my trip, Tom wanted to discuss a method of communication while I was away tripping in the event I needed help. There was no cell service in the wilds of Algonquin. You weren't going to dial up 911 and get a response. I had briefly considered a satellite emergency device, but you first purchased the device and then subscribed to the service. It was too expensive for a one time use, in my opinion. Also, there was the point of me wanting to do this completely without contact for the complete adventure aspect of it, saying goodbye on day one and then arriving back four days later.

Both Tom and I are licensed amateur radio operators and he insisted it wouldn't be much for me to pack a portable radio and a wire antenna so I could contact him. Initially I refused. It actually wasn't until this very morning while we sat having breakfast before I left that I agreed to it. At first, Tom said he would leave his radio on all the time and I could just call if I needed help. That seemed reasonable. I packed the radio and antenna. Then, as I was loading the canoe, further discussion resulted in my agreeing to calling each morning at 7am and each evening at 5pm for a brief contact.

It was coming up to 5pm. I pulled the telescoping fishing rod that Tom had rigged up with wire for my antenna, extended it into the air and attached the radio, turned it on to the frequency we decided to use on 2 metre band. When my Fitbit said 5pm, I triggered the button and called.

The protocol is to announce the callsign belonging to the person you are calling twice, followed by your own callsign. In my case, it went like this: "VE3YTN, VE3YTN, this is VE3QSN portable". The person responds with your callsign and their own, like this: "VE3QSN, this is VE3YTN", and the discussion ensues after identification.

It worked! We kept it brief. I didn't want to be chatting away for a length of time which would take me out of the moment and disturb the quiet. He sounded happy to hear I had made it to the first destination. It was amazing that while there was no service to be had out here leaving trippers totally on their own, I was able to easily touch base with the small transmitter and a fishing rod antenna!

I needed to eat. I was ravenous having not eaten since breakfast, but first I needed to treat some water so I could safely prepare my food. This two-step method would take 30 minutes. In the meantime, I pulled out a 2oz mini bottle of scotch to sip on. I rarely drink, but a friend mentioned to me how nice it might be to have a shot once camp was set up after a full day of paddling and I had to agree with them as the first sips warmed my lips and heated my throat. Unbeknownst to my husband, I had raided the liquor cabinet and found three mini bottles of scotch; one for each night.

Tonight's meal was Pork Jambalaya with Rice. Add boiling water, close the foil pouch, wait for ten to fifteen minutes and, voila - lunch and dinner, all in one. I counted down the minutes in anticipation of a satiating meal.

Dinner wasn't at all what I expected. Usually it goes that when you are out in the middle of nowhere, any food can taste really, really good – memorable, even, until you go home and try to bring that same enjoyment by making the same meal…and it never meets the mark. Ever. This time, however, it didn't even taste good out in the middle of nowhere. This was totally unexpected as I had purchased the best and fully believed it would be enjoyable. I could barely swallow it. The rice was still crunchy. Everything tasted fake. I chewed slowly, wondering how I was going to manage to eat this entire package of two meals when I was struggling on my third mouthful. The fact I was eating it right out of the package didn't add anything to the meal experience, either, but I had decided not to bring a dish to eat from in order to save space and weight in my backpack. Every little extra counted.

Two more spoons and I was done. I just couldn't force myself to eat it. This was very surprising to me as I am not a fussy eater whatsoever.

Everything you do out on a trip like this has an impact, and my not eating very much of my combination lunch and dinner meant not only was I left hungry but now I had a hydrated packet of food that I would have to fit into my bear canister and it would be added weight to carry around the rest of the trip.

My utensil was cleaned, water purification kits put together and everything was packed away when it began to rain. That's okay. In preparation for such an event, I had brought a tarp. The rain pattered on the tarp while I sat underneath slowly sipping the last of the little scotch bottle and feeling like I could handle anything. The lake was patterned from the rain, changing as the drops became more insistent. When the patter become louder, I took down the clothesline with my wet towel. I wrung it out as best I could and tossed it in the tent next to my backpack.

Sitting there, looking down the length of the lake which hadn't seen any traffic other than me and my canoe, I was thinking how if I got scared now, I couldn't just pack up and go back. It wouldn't be long until darkness closed in, especially with these heavy clouds, and it would be impossible to pack up camp, paddle and do two portages to get back to Kioshkokwi Lake. This was simply an awareness and didn't bother me at all. I was still in this. It was a good feeling.

Soon the boundary between daylight and darkness became less defined, and I was anxious to get my food canister put back in the forest. I had no desire to clamber through a dark forest where nighttime creatures watched my every move as I secured my food. I brushed my teeth, put my toiletries in with the food along with my empty scotch bottle and took my big yellow container into the trees. Once I was under the canopy, the patter of rain was replaced with dripping. Every needle of every coniferous tree held a large drop of water, all of which were eager to drop at the least little provocation. I caught a branch with my head and as it passed behind me, it delivered a good sized trickle down the back of my neck.

It was hard to imagine, but although it was quiet where I had set up near the shore, it was even quieter amongst the trees. Now that the ground was wet, my footsteps fell silent. I stopped to inhale the pure and soul cleansing scent of the forest, closing my eyes, breathing deep and trying to notice if there were other smells before heading back to my site.

The rain couldn't decide between coming in as a light shower, with the surface of the lake gently absorbing the sporadic drops, or a heavier, persistent rain which made the drops on the water unrecognizable as separate. Over and over the texture of the water changed with the intensity of the rain. I watched as it passed by, ending as quickly as it began.

Sometimes there was no noise at all except for the crickets singing once the rain stopped and sometimes the wind talked through the trees. The breeze soothed when it brushed past my face and playfully tousled my hair. I entertained myself watching small wavelets kiss the shoreline then quickly retreat to run back to deeper water. I continued watching the patterns on the water; the footprint of the wind as it scuffed the surface. I marvelled at some trees that grow far taller than the others, towering above the treeline, brave souls. Those amazing and majestic white pines; the tallest trees in Algonquin Park and Ontario's official tree. Gradually it all disappears with the last of the light.

I was in my tent early due to the rain that seemed to arrive with more urgency than before, and throughout the night wave after wave of thunderstorms rolled through. I could hear each storm approaching as the wind preceded the rain, coming at first from a distant place, picking up and rushing through the trees until it engulfed me and my tent. Rain followed; an intense and determined pounding with thunder echoing across lakes and vibrating through valleys as lightning flashed in rapid succession. One thing was certain, I didn't have to worry at all about hearing any animal sounds and setting my imagination wild.

A few hours into my night and probably my fifth thunderstorm deluge, I was presented with my first challenge. Drops of water found their way through the tent fly and began to drop inside the tent intermittently. I could tell by the sound which ones were hitting the tent floor and which ones were hitting my sleeping bag. I turned on my little battery light and reached into my backpack for the foil emergency blanket I brought as a last minute addition, spreading it out on top of my sleeping bag to catch the drops. It worked perfectly and kept my sleeping bag dry, for which I was very grateful. This was the precise moment I realized it was a mistake to have brought this old tent.

The storms, and the rain, abated at about 2am and I was dry.

No Expiry

It was 3am when my light sleep was disrupted with what sounded like a convention going on outside. Canada Geese were flying down the length of the lake, honking the entire time. It seemed like an endless parade, with periodic gaps before more honking grew louder as the birds approached this end of the lake. At least two, maybe three, geese rested on my campsite for quite a while, softly honking to each other, the sound emanating from the same spot close by, as though they were chatting around a campfire. I was surprised how active geese could be at night, but these birds have good reason. Geese don't soar and ride those warm daytime updrafts known as thermals like raptors do. Geese get up and go, from point A to point B. Thermals just mess them up, particularly when flying in V formation and the flock is relying on the air turbulence from the lead bird to help them conserve energy. It didn't sound to me like any of these birds were interested in conserving energy tonight. This was a migration party. Where the day had been so quiet, the night most certainly was not.

What sleep I did get on night number one probably amounted to between 3 and 4 1/2 hours in total. I woke early, around 5am, to the sound of a moose wading deliberately in the water along the shore in the slow and easy way a mammal weighing up to 700 kg and over 2 metres tall at the shoulder can afford to do. I zipped open the tent window with painstaking care trying to resist the urge to fling it open in haste and risk scaring the majestic beast away. My tongue between my teeth in deep concentration, I inched the zipper open tooth by tooth, all the while imagining the sight that would soon be mine and what a crown jewel in my trip on my very first night out to see this iconic Canadian animal. The flap fell back and I looked out, but there was nothing at all to be seen other than the silver sheen of the lake. My moose was actually short little waves, remnants from the storms which lashed through last night, lapping at the shoreline in a quiet cadence. I snuggled back into my sleeping bag, smiling at how easily I had been fooled. The steady lapping sound kindly put me back to sleep.

PINCH ME, IS THIS REAL?

Life is about daring to carry out your ideas. And for me, it always comes back to the wilderness, nature, mountains ~ Reinhold Messner

My morning began at exactly 6:21am. It seems wrong to be so precise with the time when out here in the backcountry where it doesn't matter at all, and especially when I know how to tell a very close approximation of the time using the sun, a stick and the direction north - a method I learned as a teenager. Sometimes I can be a bit of a purist, but anyway the sun is not even up that early this time of year, not to mention the sky is not clear so there will be no shadow cast by a stick, a necessary component. I am wearing a fitness tracker which I consciously opted to keep on for the trip given it is dark for so much longer these days and I want to know when I wake up if it is 5am, a respectable time to get up, or 1:30am, not a respectable time to get up. Aside from that, there was the standing check-in time with Tom at 7am. I needed to know the time.

There were some small puddles of water on the floor in the low lying areas of the tent, and my foil blanket had a bit of water in the folds that otherwise would have been now soaking my sleeping bag, but all in all, not too bad and easy to clean up with my small towel, still wet from yesterday's swim. Holding my sopping wet towel that still felt heavy and moisture laden even after repeatedly wringing it out, I wondered how it was going to dry with the overcast sky and how much weight this was going to add to my backpack. I hadn't planned on carrying remnants of last nights' storms, but that's exactly what I would be doing.

The steady winds that carried on, after the storms gave up trying to make me wish I hadn't come, meant the outside of the tent was nicely dried for packing up. This was a welcome and pleasant surprise that made for relative ease of putting things together.

Purifying water is already becoming a contemplative task, watching the water trickle from the membrane, out the nozzle and into the pot. Drip…drip…drip… There is no hurrying this chore. I do learn to begin combining the mixture of chemical drops for the second treatment which has to sit five minutes at the same time so it is ready to mix into the pot of water right away, avoiding added time at the end of treatment number one. While I am waiting, I decide that today I will not label the birds or other living things I see. I will simply observe them and that way be open to seeing them as they are instead of only picking up on the behaviours I already know belong to that species. Labels can be distracting, taking us out of the moment as we struggle to identify what we see as they flit in and out of the shadows. We might miss something we have never seen if we have expectations. Less than five minutes later I see a bird cross in front of me. "Chickadee", I tell myself, labelling it confidently based on its size, shape and flight pattern…

After the dinner I tried to have last night, breakfast was amazing - comparatively speaking. Breakfast is my favourite meal of the day, by far, and I basically have the same thing every day. One third cup rolled oats (uncooked), a scoop of protein powder, nuts and fruit. Out here, though, my premeasured breakfast had raisins and walnuts in place of fresh fruit which was just too heavy to consider bringing and water instead of milk was a compromise, one of which I would not repeat again on any future trip. I thought the protein powder would make the water mixture kind of milky, at least visually, but it lacked the consistency and just didn't cut it. Still, I find myself loving my breakfast and the mug of coffee, even though I would really love for it to be tea. Along with breakfast at home, I have one square of 85% dark chocolate every day. I brought the chocolate with me, knowing I wouldn't have to worry about it melting at this time of year, and so far

I was right. What a nice touch to the morning to have that smooth, melt-in-your-mouth, satiny chocolate put a smile on my face.

The contact with Tom had been made to show I made it through the night whole and unscathed. Yes, it had been a short night in terms of sleep, but a success nonetheless. I didn't lay awake terror stricken all night and I weathered out the storms just fine. One night down, two to go.

The campsite is dismantled, packed, loaded in the canoe and it is just shortly after 9am. Before I push off from shore, I do a quick adjustment to my map which is attached to the thwart so I will have a constant visual of it. There were two portages down at the end of Mink Lake; the one I will take to Club Lake, and the other which goes to Cauchon Lake. The last thing I want to do is take the wrong portage and end up on a different lake. I wasn't too worried having always been a lover of maps and the fact I poured over this particular map many times in the months leading up to this trip. I knew where I was going. Still, making assumptions in the backcountry can lead to unintended and dangerous consequences.

The next portage is the longest one yet at 985 m (1077 yds). Although I couldn't help wondering how it was going to go, at the same time I knew it didn't really matter because regardless how difficult it might be, I was going to get it done. I couldn't decide it was too hard and tell myself I was incapable of doing it. There is no one to call and there is no delete button to return to where I started. There are simply no options out here. I had prepared for this trip for a very long time. I knew the demands that would be made of me and I was confident I would be able to meet them, yet there was the factor of the unknown. I have never done this before.

It is another hunt for the yellow sign marking the take out point for the portage. This time it is hidden from the lake, about 100 metres down a shallow and narrow grassy creek. Picturesque and serene, there was a good flow moving through. It

Portage to Club Lake

was the kind of spot you'd expect to see a regal looking moose standing up to its knees in water, surrounded by tall marshy grasses, feeding thoughtfully with a bunch of greens hanging and dripping from the sides of its mouth, however, there was no such sighting. This was perfectly okay with me because as exciting as it would be to see one up close, coming upon an animal as tall as a moose while I am sitting in a canoe way down at water level would be a little intimidating, to say the least.

The lift out spot was beautifully nestled alongside the creek, flanked by the autumn kissed foliage of shrubs and grasses and it was easy to pull right up on shore with the flat, hard packed clay-like soil and, joyfully, no rocks. There were deer hoof prints in the mud. Perfect twinned halves with sharp, defined edges indicating their freshness. I felt a kinship with Mother Nature. I was out here with the wild things that lived here. Now, had these been bear tracks on the other hand, it would have put a lump in my throat, a hand on my bear spray and a loud off-key attempt at some hit song from my repertoire. I decided not to look too hard for more tracks.

I hid my large backpack and tent well off the trail just for peace of mind as it would be a while before I got back from delivering the canoe at the next lake.

What happened next on this longer jaunt just came naturally without a whole lot of thought. I carried the canoe and small backpack until I began to tire and I set it down alongside the trail, then I went back for the large backpack and tent, returned along the trail and went beyond the canoe a good distance before setting these items down. Going back for the canoe was a nice rest before picking it up and, in leapfrog style, carrying it past the point I dropped my backpack and tent, and so on. It worked wonderfully and was far easier on my shoulders than carrying the canoe the entire distance in one go. I had to admit that I was fully impressed with myself at this point.

No Expiry

I saw what I recognized as Lady's Slipper Orchid alongside the trail. Of course the flower itself which would have been in bloom late May and early June, was long gone, but the telltale plant itself with two sturdy, long ribbed leaves reaching up from the ground then gently curling downward at the top was something I was very familiar with. We have these same lovely wild orchids in our own forest at home and I look for them every spring.

There were a lot of orange mushrooms the colour of a cooked lobster, looking like big floppy hats on top of a trumpet shaped stem. Certainly they were Lobster Mushrooms, a name given to a parasitic fungus that grows over top of an existing mushroom, engulfing it in its entirety until it can no longer be identified. This whole process sounded a bit like cannibalism, and I suppose it is. Apparently they are edible, but I wasn't about to test it out. Anyway, even if I were inclined to be that adventurous, it seems a little unsettling to me to be consuming something that is a parasite.

Another mushroom, light brown in colour, has had its head lopped off and it lays upside-down on the ground filled with rainwater. It's a perfect water receptacle for insects and birds in need of a drink. Likewise, leaves that have dropped and dried with curled edges also become little pods of water. Nature provides.

The trail was mostly flat, soft and very quiet underfoot from the layer of pine needles blanketing it. Some may think the ground is hard. Rock is hard. Earth gives a little under our step, absorbing each impact, cushioning each strike regardless who or what treads above.

It appeared out of nowhere, totally unexpected and out of place. Not some wild, furry mammal charging down the trail, heaving and frothing at the mouth, or anything else alive, but a brick. A very old brick as evidenced by the shape of it, just lying alongside the trail partially covered by a low hanging pine bough. I couldn't quite understand why it would be here on this long portage in the

Mill ruins at Club Lake

backcountry. In the first place, who would carry a brick in their already heavy backpack, and secondly, why? A short distance later, I came across a spot on the trail where some of these same bricks were deeply embedded in the wet, mushy soil aiding trippers by keeping them out of the soggy mess. Very nice, but again, who would carry bricks out here when tree branches will do the same thing? A few more steps and it all became clear as to why the bricks are here and where they came from.

There before me, in the forest, are the remains of a building. Cement walls stand defiantly even though no roof remains above. Where once there were windows, there were now rectangular openings with trees, both coniferous and deciduous, climbing out from within the confines of the building, seeking sunlight. It is a skeleton of its former self.

At the time I didn't know what the building was other than it was likely a mill, but I learned afterwards it was all the remained of the Richie Bros Lumber Mill. This mill, apparently built in the 1930's when the railway ran through here, even had its own railway car, the frame of which I did see next to the ruins. Unfortunately, the lumber mill fell victim to the Great Depression. I visualize the past as I walk about these ruins, all that remains of an earlier time when employees worked hard, long hours and the steady whine of saws buzzed through felled trees, cutting them into lumber. What walls remain stand silently as nature slowly consumes them. I hadn't seen a single human in two days. It didn't seem possible that at one time this was a busy spot along the railway.

I walk around the building, being mindful that any sharp objects such as nails or glass could be hidden in the long grass and watching my every step. There is no forest on the one side of the building which is perched high on a hill. I stop and turn away from the building to see the view and that's when I see Club Lake. I couldn't believe I had arrived already. It was very difficult to determine the distance I had travelled and where I was on the portage given my indirect, leapfrog way of carrying my gear.

My view of the lake from this high spot allowed me to take in a very steep embankment to the water and see where I would be putting in my canoe. Boulders scattered on the trail meant lots of zigzagging my way down to the beach. It would take balance and patience. That was fine. I had both.

The lake looked the exact colour of how I like my tea before I add the milk. I could see that once in the water, it would be an easy paddle through a garden of lily pads. Lily pads are the floating leaves of the water lily, found in shallow and placid waters, providing shelter for fish and frogs as well as food for wildlife. I could see how the water lilies were able to survive here, surrounded and protected from any wave action by a large swath of marsh grasses encircling the arm of the bay I was in. The tall grasses were the colour of spun gold this time of year.

Large granite boulders covered in lichens punctuated the shoreline in several spots and other nooks of marshy areas further down were easily identified by grasses and reeds. While I scanned the lake, some Mergansers broke the silence, rising up into the air to fly across the lake, just a few feet above the water, before landing again.

The worn trail down to the water was like a chute between sandy walls and large rocks with understory asserting itself along the edges. I picked my way down slowly, pausing to consider next foot placement. If I twisted my ankle, I'd be sitting waiting for at least a day for help to come and get me once I notified my husband on the radio. Planes could not land on these lakes. Help would have to come the same way I did, by paddling and portaging.

Once my canoe was safely on the shore of Club Lake, the jump rope came out and I did some clumsy jumping on the beach. The hiking boots just weren't lending themselves to jump rope. Did the wildlife wonder what it was I was doing? They likely had never seen anyone undertake this type of activity here. The knowledge that I was probably the first person to ever skip on this lake is what made it fun and that pleased me.

I turned my canoe upside-down and went back for my backpack and tent, ready to get back on the water and see what this lake was waiting to reveal to me. Many would say it was just a lake as was the other, but to those of us who would paddle its length and see where rock face plunged vertically until disappearing into inky depths, or marsh grasses swayed in a game of tag with dragonflies and the play of light on forests gave the occasional glimpse of what lay beyond, we know different. Every lake, tree and rock is distinct with its own character and feel while at the same time resonating with the whole, and it is this that draws us forward to the next one.

When everything was packed into the canoe and as I was about to stick my paddle amongst the lily pads, I remembered to check my watch and, allowing for the time I spent exploring the mill, admiring the view and jumping rope on shore, I see the entire portage from start to finish took me 1 hour and 15 minutes. This was surprising and it made me happy. It felt like I was doing this thing really well and my self-confidence was gaining altitude.

Club Lake was a small lake, much of it full of reeds with plenty of marsh grass along most of the shoreline. It was a bit to paddle through before it opened up into the lake proper. From there, it was a short distance to the end of the lake where the next portage would take me to Waterclear Lake, my destination for the day.

I paddled without hurry, scanning the shoreline, watching the sky and enjoying the feel of the wind against my face. These were the moments of awareness easily missed when traveling with others.

Just as I neared the end of the lake and entered into the grassy area on my approach to the shore where I knew the portage awaited me, my eye caught movement in the water. A small wake catching the light, speeding one way, doing an abrupt turn and going another, then disappearing and leaving an echo of rings behind on the surface. More wakes followed the path of the first. I lifted my paddle from the water and rested it across the gunwales, floating quietly.

It was a family of five otters – dipping, diving, twisting, arching, changing direction – all of them following the leader, playfully frolicking and totally oblivious to my presence. It is the very thing that makes tripping in nature so special and memorable when you come upon animals simply being themselves; not on guard, not knowing you are there witnessing them. Eventually, though, all great things come to an end and it didn't look as though those otters were ever going to stop playing, so I carried on. The very second I dipped my paddle into the water and disturbed the surface the otters quickly dove in unison, disappearing without a sound or a ripple, leaving me to wonder if they had been there in the first place.

The yellow portage marker was right where I expected to find it. The pull out was not going to be as easy as the others had been so far. Before me was an expanse of black mud pockmarked with people's footprints filled with water. There was no walking around it as it stretched the entire clearing and extended into the forest. I realize this is its natural, wet state when I see three saplings, devoid of branches, lying side by side in the mud, set in place and used by others to get their canoe and equipment to the solid ground beyond. I tested out the makeshift boardwalk without carrying anything, gently balancing on the middle round trunk, arms outstretched. The black mud oozed through the spaces between the small saplings, all of which were about 5 to 7.5 cm in diameter, and made sucking noises like it was hungry and meant to have me for a meal should I fall in. The makeshift boardwalk would have to do. At the very least, it would stop me from having mud over my ankles along with the risk of losing a hiking boot in there. I went back for my gear and my first attempt.

I managed to keep my focus and my balance, safely going back and forth without incident, and got my canoe and gear beyond the threat. Messy situation averted. This was a short portage at 350 metres. I am settled into the routine now and I don't waste any time before I begin my trek through the forest to the next lake.

I started off singing in order to alert any bears that I was coming through, so they wouldn't be surprised and in turn, surprise me. On my second day out, I think I sound pretty good.

It didn't take long to notice the portage, while relatively short, was not flat. There were inclines, there were rocks, then a further rise up and I found myself thinking that was just fine because surely the climbing part was almost done and I would soon be going down. It wasn't. No longer singing, I was puffing like Thomas the Engine as I reached the top of a hill and expected to see a leveling off, but instead there was a very sharp descent and a boardwalk that was so far down, it looked like part of a miniature railroad display. I knew I would have to take this slow and be careful not to catch the back of the canoe on the hill. While I tried to ignore it, I couldn't help but notice there was a steep hill going up on the other side.

While these things were unexpected and made going a little slower, it was all part of the adventure and I was enjoying the challenge. This was what I signed up for and it was exactly what I wanted to experience.

Eventually the canoe and all my gear were resting on the shore and I stood gazing out at yet another body of water. This was Waterclear Lake and I was expecting big things of it with such a name. I imagined crystal clear water that would be at this moment winking at me with sparkles if only the sun were shining, water so pure it would allow me to see down into the depths to admire silvery scaled fish swimming between aquatic growth on the lake bed. From the shore, the lake didn't give up its secrets.

I was hungry and once again I didn't see the sense in unpacking to access my food and spending time to purify water for lunch when this would be the lake I was stopping on for today and I would be on a site before too long.

Waterclear Lake is another long and slender lake, much like Mink Lake. Clouds are grey and heavy, reflected back in the choppy water so I don't forget they are there, hanging above me. Forest flanked one side of the lake, meeting the shoreline looking dark and impenetrable, while higher land formed the shore on the other. I selected a campsite on the high side facing southwest, just in case the sun did make an appearance, I wanted to be bathed in it. From this spot I could look both out across and down the length of the lake.

The site had not been used too much this season, if at all. Long grass grabbed at my feet as I walked and had grown over some small fallen trees, effectively hiding them. Rocks, too, were hidden in the grasses – definitely a tripping hazard and I made a mental note to pay close attention. I briefly wondered if I should forego having my scotch this evening so I'd be fully alert and cautious, but before I had even fully formed the thought I had already quickly decided everything would be fine. The decision was made without further deliberation.

Camp set up went even faster today and before I knew it, I had swung my jump rope around in the long grass and managed to jump over it several consecutive times, and I was down at the water's edge going for a swim while my water purified. I didn't spend long in the water as it was chilly, there was no sun to warm me and I was hungry, so it was in, out 15 metres and straight back to shore, not to mention I was a little startled when my knee scraped against a rock on entry. It altered the moment. I hadn't seen it. What else was down there I couldn't see?

When I was once again in warm clothes, I indulged in a handful of trail mix with some chocolate chunks in it; an impulse purchase that I had forgotten was in the bottom of my bear canister. I am so glad I splurged and bought two small packets of this ridiculously expensive snack. It tasted amazing and I know I was wearing

Campsite on Waterclear

the biggest grin on my face while I got my propane stove out to boil my precious water for dinner.

There's two more tasks to be done before I can totally relax. I want to locate the vault and also figure out where my bear canister will be placed overnight. It is easy to find the trail that leads into the forest where the vault is, but at this particular site there is a very steep climb up a hill of loose rock which is mostly overgrown with errant branches stretching across the trail grabbing at my clothes and trying to take the ball cap from my head. I haven't, to this point, stopped and checked my site before setting up but maybe I should have. It looks to me as though most people have checked out this site and bypassed it, although maybe the whole lake isn't camped on very often. I immediately recalled that people avoided this route and its longer portages. Wussies, I thought to myself.

While this steep climb isn't something I'll worry about, I think of people who are drinking and making the vertical trek in that condition. It could certainly be a bit risky. My bear canister can't sit on this grade or it will roll away into oblivion if something is nosing around it during the night. Luckily there are more level areas nearby and I spy a tree with a nice, cozy cavity for my canister to snuggle into.

The extravagant and lightweight 950 gram chair I purchased for this trip which folds into a neat little carry-all is my most fun item after my jump rope. It is yellow, orange and purple tie dye with burnt orange titanium legs, a full back and very comfortable. There is nothing better than this moment sitting in the chair, looking out at the lake while the water I boiled is now combined with dehydrated, supposed real food mixed with I don't know what else, in a foil bag and resting for 15 minutes when it will be considered edible. I have decided to be optimistic and feel confident dinner will taste far better than last night. I have been hungry since yesterday and I am really looking forward to it.

No Expiry

I crack open mini scotch bottle number two and nurse it with tiny little sips to make it last and keep the enjoyment going. I am feeling really good this far into the trip.

Finally my foil pack of Sweet and Sour Pork is ready and I dig into the foil bag. Again I am wishing I had brought a plate or bowl as it would have made eating more of an event than eating it out of the same bag it was packaged in. The meal is still a little crunchy in spots even though I was extra careful to stir it thoroughly, and there's no denying, it tastes artificial. Eating this stuff is taking some effort again today. I give myself a pep talk about how I am burning lots of extra calories each day with my portaging all this heavy stuff through the forest from lake to lake, up hills and down gullies, and I need to refuel, particularly when I'm not eating lunch, either. I really must eat this food. The talk doesn't help. I fail miserably and, just as last night, I end up with most of it untouched, adding more weight to my food canister. As it is, every time I take the lid off my canister, the smell of the uneaten meal is a constant reminder of the unpalatable food. There were now two almost full packages of hydrated food in there and I am still hungry.

Afterwards I document the day in my journal, pausing often to watch a loon that seems to really favour the section of lake directly in front of me. Serenely, it swims a distance, dives out of sight, then reappears in a different spot, systematically swimming back and forth, dipping its head beneath the surface, scanning for food, moving fluidly. This is flow in nature. Every time it dives I play a game, trying to determine where it will come up. I am wrong every time.

While I journal, I look across the water to study the trees on the other side as if their branches are laden with the words I seek, ripe for the picking.

There is wind in the trees but it's sporadic, and when it stops altogether there is no sound at all and I wonder for a brief moment if I have lost my hearing. Silence brings awareness tenfold. Soon I notice the lake lapping lazily, tossing itself in sloppy, haphazard form against the shore, yet it makes no sound. It reaches the exact same water mark each time, never going beyond the wet mark set before, never coming in short. The only other movement comes from the sulky clouds overhead, dragging their bellies across the sky.

I begin to think about the ability to hear and what it might be like if I had never been able to but suddenly I could. I imagine all the sounds, on top of each other, excited to introduce themselves to me for the first time; one beginning before the other is finished while yet another sound is in the background and perhaps I move in astonishment, my foot making a sound on gravel while a bird simultaneously breaks into song. All of it beautiful, but also overwhelming as my brain would try to deal with each sound having never heard it before – determining if it is safe or if it's a warning, guessing what it is and me turning this way and that to locate the source of each.

I also think about the fact I am here, by myself, yet not alone, together with the natural world. This wasn't foreign to me – the trees, lakes, forest, sun, wind and rain. We all know these elements intimately that make life possible here on earth.

My senses seem to switch from hearing to feeling. It feels comfortable in this place. I held the silence, honoured it, felt my soul lighten a little as I slipped my hand into the shallows and luxuriated in the texture of the water and the coolness of it as it closed over my hand.

When we break it all down to the basic structures that support us, it comes to this simplicity, yet as simple as it is, putting it into a feeling or capturing it in a phrase that can be shared as an all-encompassing understanding seems elusive, if not impossible. It needs to be experienced firsthand after a stripping away of the constant thought carousel that plagues us, pulling us back and keeping us away from mindfulness – the key to understanding.

I am meant to be here. Everything is as it should be.

No Expiry

The loon calls out, its haunting sound long and unhurried, bookended on either side by silence. I hope this will be followed by another call. There is no need for the loon to call out again, however, because now, swimming up the lake is another loon. Not an adult, but this year's chick. It powers quickly towards the parent, who, upon seeing it approach is satisfied, turns its back to it and continues fishing. The juvenile almost reaches it and then the adult dives, leaving the youngster alone. The little one begins to make little chirping noises as it circles about on the surface where the parent disappeared. Soon the parent emerges a little further away and again, the youngster motors eagerly towards it, but this time when it reaches the parent, they touch beaks and my heart melts at this show of affection.

A bit later, the parent is successful in catching a small fish and brings it to the juvenile who gobbles it up. All this time I've been watching, I haven't seen the young one dive even though it is surely capable by now.

Loons build nests from May to as late as mid-July and will typically lay one or two eggs. Baby loons become fledglings around 12 weeks of age so this little one must be nearly there. I'm taking a guess it hatched near the end of June. I only see one parent and because I know it is both that take turns looking after baby, it is likely one parent has already left for the ocean where it will winter in open water. The lakes here freeze solid from December through March, so the whole family must migrate. The remaining parent will be leaving soon and it may even leave before the youngster, who could possibly hang around by itself in the lake it was born on for a few weeks before flying out.

I sit here marvelling at nature and how it works just so. It definitely is a gift to be able to feel its rhythm here and be witness to it.

I didn't collect branches and twigs for a fire. Everything is saturated still, and I am enjoying the sweetness of the air.

There hasn't been a single soul to be seen yesterday or today. Do I miss that? No, and it looks as though I am going to have this lake to myself tonight, too. Well, excepting the loons, of course.

THERE'S A CHANGE OF PLANS...

Twenty years from now you will be more disappointed by the things that you didn't do than by the ones you did do. So throw off the bowlines. Sail away from the safe harbour. Catch the trade winds in your sails. Explore. Dream. Discover ~ Mark Twain

Oh boy, it was cold last night. I didn't learn just how cold it was until I got back from my trip and found out it had gone down to 2 C . All I know is that I had fragmented sleep, waking up repeatedly being cold. Both nights I have gone to bed fully clothed with jacket, even going as far as still wearing my knife on my belt. I know you are warmer in a sleeping bag if you sleep naked but I couldn't bring myself to do that in case I needed to exit quickly during the night in the event I had a bear visit my camp.

Once again I pulled out my foil emergency blanket and laid it on top of my sleeping bag, but this time for warmth and not for the purpose of keeping me dry. The foil blanket did its job and stopped me from shivering, something I felt on the verge of. Its usefulness also went above and beyond when I heard some scurrying and then something sniffing just outside my tent. I simply had to move and the crinkling noise of the foil sent whatever it was running into the underbrush. Having had a similar incident on my trial run camping trip at Arrowhead Provincial Park in June, I know it was most likely a racoon. Bears don't scurry. Again, I was surprised at my lack of concern.

Soaking up warmth

As I lay there awake during the long night, I listened to a Barred Owl hooting into the darkness. It is a sound I recognize easily with its quick hooo-hooo-hooo-hooooaw, finished off with a rolling sound at the end. This was the very experience I was looking for and I found the call comforting in its familiarity. Much later, I have no idea what time it was during the endless night, came the mournful howl of a wolf. It was beautiful as it rose to a peak, held steady, and then fell. I visualized the animal, snout pointed up towards the sky, ears lying back following the line of its body and eyes gently closed as if concentrating on the purity of the sound being emitted. The howl only happened once and I didn't hear any response from other wolves. It was also distant and came from the other side of the lake, so this, too, was comforting to me and allowed me to enjoy the experience fully without anxiety.

For the second night in a row I hear the geese, and although they carry on squawking and honking down the length of the lake, it doesn't last as long as last night's show on Mink Lake.

At 5:20am I am up. Even though it is still dark I can feel as much as see that everything is socked in with fog as cool mist lays thick against my face as soon as I climb out of the tent. This, of course, is due to the cold night and the fact the lake is much warmer. I want to move around to get good and warm but this site is not the safest for navigating in daylight let alone darkness. I slept with my wool toque on but I take it off and pull my buff up from my neck and tug it over my head like a periscope. I stick close to my tent, taking in the morning, marching on the spot and doing modified jumping jacks without the jump until it is light enough to begin walking around safely.

As daylight asserts itself and illuminates the gracefully moving fog that hugs the surface of the lake as it swirls to music I cannot hear, I see the loons are there. They feel like friends now that I have seen them for the second time. They are in no rush and silently float, ever watchful. I wonder how long they have been there. What time do they get up? Has the parent already been hunting for breakfast?

It isn't long until I have purified water, set it to boil on my propane stove and I'm holding onto my mug of coffee as though there is a high risk someone might come along and take it from me. The heat I feel permeating through my gloved hands is more welcome than the beverage itself. Nonetheless, I do appreciate the coffee and enjoy it, trying not to think of tea. My prepackaged and measured oats, protein powder, nuts and raisins in a baggie with added water is ready and waiting but I am reluctant to let go of the hot cup and, besides, I am watching my friends on the water. This breakfast is already growing tired on day two. I eat oats every single day and love them, but quite honestly, substituting water for milk was a big mistake. There is no body or taste to water and it just seems my oats got rained on and became soggy. I'm also tired of eating out of bags. It seems like practical overdone and not enjoyable at all, which is a big surprise to me. It makes me realize how small things, that seem insignificant, can have a big impact - such as a plastic bowl certainly would have. The difference being I would feel as if I were actually having a meal as opposed to scooping food out of a flimsy bag which strikes me as being as pleasurable as eating a pill for a meal. Definitely food would be done differently on any future wilderness adventure.

My bright red mug is emptied leisurely while I watch the loons become more active. Once again it becomes a game, the parent diving and me, as well as the juvenile, trying to guess where it will surface again. The youngster turns this way and that, I scan back and forth in straight lines and the parent takes its time. I am enjoying this game as the fog floats upwards like a veil being lifted, presenting the day, and it looks like a good one. It is still mighty cold but there is blue sky between the breaks in the clouds – the first hint at sun I have had since I began this adventure. I quickly pushed the idea of having a second cup of coffee out of my head knowing that would just add another hour before setting off on my day and turn to the task of packing up camp.

No Expiry

When I climb up the grassy embankment back to my campsite after looking out over the water watching fog dances with loons it is a noticeable and sudden contrast. When I faced the water there wasn't anything artificial. Everything was natural and connected, a direct line to my senses. When I faced my campsite, however, there was distraction. An immediate chaos of colour, materials and items lined up on a log like a conveyor belt. Water purification kits, propane stove, baggie from breakfast, a spoon, my journal, a cooking pot, toilet paper, dishcloth, bear canister, toothbrush and toothpaste, hand sanitizer, and a second set of woollen gloves - everything in array of colours from blue, yellow, red, green, grey and black. It was a bit mind-blowing, going from the serene advancement of dawn to a messy array of "necessities". I became annoyed standing there looking at all this and was compelled to speak my mind.

"If I am a minimalist, why do I have so much shit?"

Of course, no one was there to answer, and clearly I did need all of these things in order to drink safely, boil water for coffee and be hygienic. Nothing before me was unnecessary. I had gone over everything time and time again to make sure I wasn't taking anything with me that would go unused and create added weight. Part of the discontent was the sprawl of everything, being a person who used things and then immediately put them away this wasn't bringing comfort, but again, with a backpack that I packed systematically, things had to remain unpacked until the last minute.

As soon as I began to pack up, everything went smooth and orderly. Yes, there was all this "stuff", but it all had its place in my backpack and in no time at all it was sitting alongside my canoe waiting to be loaded and secured.

Both loons swam off down the lake as I pack up my canoe, the furthest I have seen them go since I arrived late yesterday afternoon, and they have disappeared by the time my paddle shatters the mirror reflection of the sky in Waterclear Lake and I'm off. Tiny mauve fall asters enjoying their little micro-climate between the shoreline rocks have their little faces turned towards me as if to say goodbye.

It was going to be an easy day, the easiest one yet. The plan was to do just one portage of 345 metres into the very next lake, which is Whitebirch Lake, and stay there for my last night. The clouds were spaced even further apart now and the sun was taking command of the day. I would have most of the day to play, contemplate and watch the sun track across the sky. I was looking forward to this as my energy level was very low. Even with paddling, I couldn't seem to get thoroughly warmed.

The stillness of mornings typically give way to daytime breezes as the earth's surface heats up. This is what gives voice to the trees. In summer months it's the deciduous trees, draped in their seasonal chlorophyll absorbing garb, talking amongst themselves as the message of the moment follows around the lake in waves of elegant dance. They bend towards each other in playful verse, sometimes in unison and other times completely out of synch. It's hard to feel alone amongst the kinship of trees.

I locate the yellow portage sign easily, wrapped around the tree relaying all the pertinent information. Waterclear Lake to Whitebirch Lake 345 metres. The landing was not ideal with boulders nestled in long grasses just as my campsite had been. It seemed to be the theme of this lake.

The portage may have been short, but I found it nasty. Steep inclines, steep declines, rocks to step over, on top of and around, not to mention gnarly roots as thick as arms across the trail giving the impression of a forbidden passage. I remembered to sing on the trail to alert bears way before we were within viewing distance of each other, even though I was hardly in the mood. I had my eyes glued to the ground to find where my next step placement would be so there was no scanning my environment for animals except when I came to a stop. With such a short portage before I could relax for the day, I was motivated to power on as much as I didn't feel like it.

There was a feeling of elation when through the trees and understory I saw a green blue surface glittering in sunlight. Of course it was the next lake and it beckoned. It lured. It tells me I've almost made it. To get there, though, I needed to play hopscotch while carrying my canoe over the boulder garden between me and the water.

I paddled against a variable headwind right down the middle of Whitebirch Lake, which, like Mink Lake and Waterclear Lake, is long and narrow. The wind is okay, though, because the sun is shining and is trying its best to warm me up. I paddled happily and studied the landscape. The lake looks different from the others with flatter landform down one side of it. I was loving the feel of the sun. The wind I handled easily by putting a little more power in my stroke.

The wind knows many nuances, some difficult to interpret. At times a breeze can be hard to define when it uses the trees as an instrument in its orchestra. It can be like a playmate you were looking for earlier, now sneaking up and around, passing through neighbouring trees until it is upon you. It can have you believing rain is coming through the forest toward you when the wind is only coming on its own and in the next moment have you searching high and low for the rapids you hear that aren't really there, sounding like water brushing over the rocks when really it is just leaf frolic.

I knew from going over the map in advance of this trip there were four places available to set up camp on this lake. Pulling the paddle out of the water and laying it across the canoe in front of me, I checked my map for the locations. Right away the canoe turned sideways in the stiff breeze and now with the broad side facing the wind, it effortlessly began to push me back at a pace faster than I had been able to paddle forward. I could see ahead where the first campsite was and immediately I was disappointed to see it heavily shaded with towering trees right to the shoreline. It wasn't the place I wanted to spend the day and set up camp. I wanted sunshine and warmth. I dipped the paddle back in the water, made up the distance I had lost and carried on. I found the next two sites were also dark with shade and I bypassed them, too. There was one more possibility down near the end of the lake. If it wasn't any better, I'd simply have to decide which one of them was the best.

This lake wasn't doing anything to make me feel warm and fuzzy by this point, but then something happened which made me feel very uncomfortable. I was overtired, marginally grumpy, if there existed such a thing, hungry as usual and burning energy paddling against the wind, but even so – there was something else about it and I couldn't put my finger on it. Seeing as Whitebirch Lake was narrow, I was paddling right down the middle so I wouldn't have to worry about rocks or deadwood lurking just under the surface as one might expect along the shoreline.

The sun tracks on a low trajectory across the sky this time of year and it meant the angle with which it hit the lake's surface illuminated the first few feet of water before it was lost to the dark green depths. I couldn't see the bottom. It just looked deep. All of a sudden, my eyes spotted a rock jutting up from out of those depths just a few feet to the right of me and it was only at most 5 cm below the surface. What I could see of the rock was shaped like a pillar, a light brown colour near the top, then growing darker further down until I could no longer see it below where the sun's light no longer reached. I know I gasped out loud. Then, wondering what I was paddling over top of, I looked to my left and saw two more such pillar shaped rocks, also just sitting quietly below the surface. These rocks were like long, narrow fingers standing on their own rising up from the depths of the lake. I will be honest here and tell you these rocks freaked me out. Had I gone over any one of them in my canoe, I could have easily got hung up on it and tipped. Sure, I was wearing my lifejacket and, yes, all my gear was tied down but imagine the resistance of swimming fully clothed, with heavy hiking boots on, dragging an upside-down canoe with all this stuff hanging from underneath it to the shore. It would be a difficult enough task even if the canoe was empty. Thinking through the "what if", I realized that even once I had arrived at shore, turning the canoe over would likely mean I would have to duck underwater to release the tied gear and remove it first. Everything would be soaked through, including myself, boots and jacket which would not be an ideal situation when I still had a night to go.

It was then and there I decided I really didn't like Whitebirch Lake. I knew I was not myself right then, but still, I had bad vibes about it.

As I paddled down the rest of the lake I was wrestling in my mind whether I would stay on this lake at all, even though that had been the plan, or would I push on? If I pushed on it would mean the longest portage of my trip was next on tap at 1300 metres. That seemed a little daunting given how I was feeling, but I began to worry if tonight was as cold as last night then I would be really energy depleted by tomorrow morning and having to face such a long portage in that state may not be a fun way to begin the day.

I hadn't yet decided what I was going to do when I got near the end of the lake. I pulled the canoe up to the shore at a great natural landing spot and stopped at the last campsite to look at my map and make my final decision. The campsite was really quite large and covered in a cushion of pine needles, which was pleasant to walk on. It was a really nice and open spot, especially after coming from one I could hardly walk around on for the vegetation and rocks. I jumped rope there, fully enjoying the flat, unencumbered space and the soft, cushioned landing. Afterwards, I climbed up onto a tall rock poking out of the water at the shore to look at my map. The lake lapped the shore in a steady tempo, reminding me why I was here in the first place. I sat quietly and allowed myself to be pulled into the rhythm, watching the sun play on each small wave.

When you think of trees with sunlight falling on them you never think of the underside of leaves having the opportunity, but here at the shore I look above me and the leaves are catching the sunlight reflected from the water and there is a light show going on as ripples of light play on each leaf. I find myself lost in the moment, spellbound by the flickering of sunlight in an unlikely spot where it seems it shouldn't exist, yet it does. It is like being gifted something not many have seen.

The portage was very close, just around a nearby point, and it seemed to be calling my name. The thing was, if I committed to doing this 1300 metre portage right now, that wouldn't be the end of my day because the lake it takes me to, Little Mink Lake, is small and there is no camping on it. It would therefore mean a further portage of 635 metres to get to the next lake, which was Kioshkokwi Lake. There are many backcountry sites on Kioshkokwi, a much larger lake, and it is the final lake of my journey, coming full circle and closing off the route from where I began. If I chose to do this, it would mean no portages at all in the morning. I would be simply paddling up the lake to the campground. This had its appeal for a few reasons – I'd get it done and have the hard and lengthy portaging part behind me, spend a relaxing evening without worry about being tired in the morning and tomorrow have a leisurely breakfast of oats in a bag with water and coffee followed by a paddle up the lake with no further portages. There was also the fact tomorrow was our 44th wedding anniversary and Tom and I had plans to drive out to civilization for a fish and chip dinner. The thought of arriving back with time to have a nice, long shower and then sharing a cup of tea, or two, with my husband beforehand was an exceptionally pleasant thought.

At first I struggled with feeling a little disappointed because I had taken a lot of time to plan this trip out and now I was going to change it because of... what? Bad vibes? Yes. I decided rather than stress about it, I was going for it. Do all my portages today, remembering that every portage was three trips back and forth, and camp tonight on my final lake. There was nothing to be disappointed about. I would still have done the trip in its entirety, paddled the same lakes, carried my stuff on the same portages and camped three nights in the backcountry and spent four days out on my own.

Now that I knew what I was doing, I was back in the canoe and heading towards the long portage.

No Expiry

When I edged around the point and caught sight of the bright yellow sign identifying the portage, I had one more check in with myself in case I wanted to change my mind. No. I was solid. I beached the canoe, ignored my fatigue and prepared for the trek, unfastening my gear, dropping it on the ground, jamming the paddle under the seat and moving the yoke into position for portaging. The yoke is a contoured piece of wood running across the canoe with a shape that cups the shoulders and a first quarter moon cut-out where it rests along the back of the neck for ease of carrying. With a canoe this short in length, the yoke needs to be moved from centre to allow room for being seated and paddling, then moved back to centre in order to portage your vessel overhead. This is done by loosening wingnut screws and getting it into position by pushing it along underneath the gunwales.

Backpack and tent stored out of sight behind a large, recently fallen pine at the start of the portage, canoe ready to be thrust into position over my shoulders as it had been done countless times on this trip, I took a deep breath and eyed the trail as it disappeared into the trees, winding upwards. Of course it was upwards. That's okay, I told myself. I was ready to begin.

I was taking my time and being kind to myself, just slowly picking my way through the forest, aware of the smells and feeling each footstep connect with Mother Earth. A decent sized hill had me just focusing on one step at a time: heel, roll, toe, push off – easy and rhythmic. The canoe balanced nicely over my head and didn't give me any trouble on the incline, certainly a benefit of three days of carrying. Reaching the top of one long hill, I found I wasn't even winded – surprising to me after starting off my day running on empty.

I was practicing my leap frog method of portaging my stuff and was carrying my canoe past where I had last put down my backpack and tent when just ahead on the trail was this great expansive bare spot of lovely, flat bedrock and the sun had sourced a route through the trees to shine right on it. When I reached the spot and saw the full on sunshine bathing the rock surface invitingly, I simply couldn't resist. My canoe came down and I placed it carefully alongside the trail just in case someone came along and it might be in their way, and I laid down on that rock right in the middle of the trail. I could feel the warm breath of the sun as it reached out to meet me. Overhead, small puffs of cloud skittled across the opening between the trees like a conveyor belt, appearing, disappearing but politely not passing in front of the sun. I envisioned them getting caught on the treetops and leaving a cottony chunk of themselves behind. I suddenly felt a little giddy thinking how ridiculous it was to put the canoe on the side of the trail in case someone came along as I hadn't seen anyone at all since I began the trip and even if someone did come along they would still have to wait for me to get my sorry butt out of the way, or at least sit to rest after laughing at finding a grey haired woman alone, lying on her back on a rock in the middle of the forest. More likely they would be joyous to find that I was alive and not a person they found on the trail who had passed to the other side, putting a damper on their trip.

The sun baked rock was warm underneath, seeping into my backside and making me relax. It felt like a comforting hug as the sun passed its medicinal benefits on to my weary body. I was a depleted battery lying on a solar charging mat. I lay there for probably half an hour, looking straight up, just watching the sky, seeing the full height of the trees, the tips of which I cannot ever hope to touch, listening to the forest sounds and enjoying the moment. I am wondering, too, about what this view looks like from up there looking down, from the perspective of a bird of prey soaring gracefully as it rides the thermals never needing to flap its wings, only needing to steer with its tail; a little tilt to the right, a little tilt to the left, simply gliding to its destination using the wind.

It was a glorious recharge. How remarkable that I could find a rock so comfortable! It seemed to fit the curve of my back perfectly. I know I had a smile on my face when I eventually got up, picked up my canoe and trekked on. I felt fully rejuvenated and energized, ready to go.

It took a while, but eventually I came to the forest intersection I had thought of as so urban that first day only this time I was approaching from what I had at the time considered the off ramp when I had passed it. I stopped at the intersection, put down my canoe and headed back for my backpack.

With my longest portage behind me, I rested on the shore of Little Mink Lake and took the time to pull my kits out of the backpack to purify some water and have a good, long drink. I was good and hungry, but I was really, really thirsty. I grabbed a handful of the trail mix with chocolate chunks in it to snack on. Before me was a quick paddle down this small lake and then the very last portage of my journey. I wasn't in a rush. I wanted to take in every moment, even though I knew I would be setting up camp very late in the day. This wasn't a race. I had put off this trip for years and it was in danger of not happening had I not stopped coming up with excuses out of fear and just got down to doing it. Now that I was closing the loop and ending this trip I wanted to make sure I experienced everything there was. I was feeling sad that this would be my last night out in the wilderness.

One thing about going on a wilderness trip in September is there are far fewer mosquitoes, if any. If you have never had the experience of a mosquito flying directly into your ear and buzzing around intermittently just to let you know it is still in there, and stuck, then you need to spend more time outdoors. For such a tiny insect it sure is distracting for a good hour or so until it finally succumbs…in your ear. Later, when you are poking about in there with a cotton swab you realize how ridiculous it would sound to tell someone you pulled two legs out of your ear. Family and friends may become concerned with how much time you are spending alone out in nature. I am speaking from experience.

I made the paddle across Little Mink Lake a meandering one, stopping to look at some rock cliffs along shore, poking into a little bay along the way, inhaling the scents of the forest and floating near shore looking down at all the plant life growing on the bottom gracefully reaching up. Even with all the side trips, it wasn't long before I had landed at the other end with the last portage staring at me. I pulled the canoe up on shore, lifted it overhead yet again and headed off into the forest after climbing up the steep hill from shore. I had travelled this portage on the way out and I knew exactly how it went. There was the swampy area, crossing over the abandoned railway track, down the hill, the river, gurgling and tripping over itself, racing to Kioshkokwi Lake, and then Kioshkokwi itself. The final lake.

Just after I crossed over the railway line is where I came across the first human beings I'd seen since Tuesday morning when I left. A huge group passed me, heading to Little Mink Lake, with six canoes and 12 people and a dog that wasn't happy with me being on the portage. Thankfully, he was on a leash because he barked, snarled and raised up on his hind legs as they passed. We didn't really say much to each other as I had the canoe over my head and stepped aside to let them pass. I just hoped when the dog was walking past my backpack and tent further down the trail that he didn't cock his leg and pee on it.

It was almost dinner time when I had my canoe packed up after the portage and ready to head into the lake. I had the marsh to paddle through to get into the lake proper and I remembered I wanted to keep to the right side in order to avoid those shallow spots where there were sandbars and a few submerged tree limbs.

As I came out into the lake, I was met with a stiff wind once I was no longer protected by the marsh grasses. Kioshkokwi Lake, often a challenging paddle unless it is early morning or late evening when it is normally in a subdued mood, was currently in a mood, which was not subdued.

I knew which campsite I wanted. A number of times I had paddled over to it and just sat there imagining what it would be like to be on a solo trip and setting up camp here, watching the sun set and staying up to watch the night sky push daylight aside and produce the constellations and the Milky Way for my viewing pleasure. Each time I had stopped at that backcountry site I vowed I would do my solo trip. It seemed fitting that I should stay on that spot.

I paddled into the waves as long as I could and then angled against them to get to my destination. I didn't want the waves hitting me directly on the side which would make the canoe a little less stable. As I came within view of the campsite, I was disappointed to see someone was on it already. Not surprising as it is a very nice site overlooking the lake and facing south so sun in the morning is yours as are spectacular sunsets in the evening. I knew there was another one tucked into a little bay further along so I paddled toward that one and, again, found it to be taken. I turned around and headed back to the train trestle where I knew there was another site nearby. The sun was low in the sky, flirting with the horizon, when I pulled on shore at the campsite. It was very steep up to it but it was a good site. I set up quickly and began preparations for dinner. I was famished and it had been a mammoth day, more than the anticipated easy 345 metre portage and a day of play and contemplation on Whitebirch Lake. I was glad I had made this decision, though, because had I stayed back on that lake as scheduled, I would have questioned my decision throughout the day until it was too late to do anything about it. Hence, the freedom and lightness of the day would have been compromised anyway. It was all worth it for the feeling of calm I had.

I pulled out the fishing rod, extended it and made contact with Tom, never mentioning that I was on the same lake as he was and not on Whitebirch Lake as planned.

As the day had been dry and free of rain, I put on my moccasins so I could feel the earth beneath my feet, appreciating its softness where there was sand, its support where there were rocks and the bareness of the trail to the thunder box. Out came my chair and was together in no time, supporting me and allowing me to lean back and view the end of the day while I ate what I could of dinner and sipped on my scotch. It had become partially overcast now, but the sun, as it settled in the west, sent up a warm glow at the last minute like a fizzling firework everyone had mistakenly thought was done. Merlot and burnt orange clouds framed the setting sun against a peach sky as its last rays reached high enough to

Last night out
Kioshkokwi

paint the bottoms of clouds a cotton candy pink; the forest below, shades of the darkest greens, growing darker by the minute; the lake, like an indigo and silver platter, carrying a near perfect reflection of the sky. How is it even possible to answer when someone asks me what my favourite colour is?

I was feeling very peaceful and pleased as I looked out on the lake, reflecting on this trip so far and thinking just how close I was to finishing it up.

DAY FOUR, IT'S A WRAP

When the happenings of the world peel off and fall away, and all you know is the sky, land, water and nature at its very core, you can't help but become one with it all, as you should, because we are, after all, nature, too. ~ Sheila Nollert

It rained during the night. Hard. It was totally unexpected after an evening spent looking up into the sky imagining all those before me who looked up in the same way and marvelled at those shimmering pinpoints of light in the night sky. There was no sign the wet weather was making its way toward me. I didn't get the memo.

It started to come down just after 11pm and continued for 3 or 4 hours. My tent, once again, let it in. As it seems with all things, after you have given the okay the first time, each consecutive time there is less resistance to the thing happening again. The drops permeated the tent fabric easier than before, lined up overhead with uniform precision along the seam and proceeded to drip on me. Once again I reached for the foil emergency blanket and yet again it saved my sleeping bag, and me, from getting wet. It occurred to me I had used it every night - twice for rain, once for cold. My nights could well have been miserable without it. I will always recommend trippers to throw one in their backpack.

I would describe myself as a positive person, accepting and working with what I have been given, but I have to say that I did groan when the rain came down. I was disappointed, perhaps even annoyed. There had been quite a bit of rain on

Morning coffee

my trip, but even so, there were so many more positives. I hadn't once got caught in a solid downpour while paddling, unless you want to count my paddling technique at the start that had me totally drenched from the hips down, and I had been able to set up camp, cook meals, and take down camp without any rain.

I burrowed down into my sleeping bag and tried to ignore the deluge happening on the other side of my tent.

Sleep must have eventually found me because I woke up with a start at 4:30am when I heard a loud noise. I was immediately on high alert. It wasn't the grunt of a bear but could it have been a moose? It sounded loud, and it did sound like a noise made from a living thing rather than, say, a tree falling. As I lay there listening for more noise to ascertain what I was dealing with and hearing absolutely nothing at all, I began to wonder if I had really heard the noise or dreamed it, or perhaps I was breathing through my lips and made a noise that woke me up. I unzipped the tent, clambered outside and stood there looking around but there was nothing to see. No bear, no moose, not even a mouse was stirring as far as I could tell. The silence was total as I stood in the darkness, small battery operated lantern in one hand, bear spray in the other. This may sound like a rather brave thing to do but it is very different when there is only yourself to rely on. With someone else along, you simply tap them on the shoulder, tell them you heard something and they need to go check it out while you hold the flashlight for them, or better yet, stay in bed. When you are on your own, you set fear aside because you are the person who has to deal with it. Anyway, I think it is far scarier to be in a tent not being able to determine what is happening outside while your imagination goes into overdrive, not to mention getting out while the getting is good. Tents only have one exit.

There is nothing going on out here in the dark. There are no further noises and the hair on the back of my neck was not standing up in warning. At this point there was no sense in going back to bed. The rain had stopped and there was the calmness that comes with the predawn hours. Numerous small pools of water patterned my tent floor, but eventually I found a dry spot and pulled my sleeping bag around me to write in my journal by the soft light of my little lantern. I left the tent door folded back so I could look out and watch the different levels of daylight: astronomical dawn, which comes well before sunrise when the sun lies 18 degrees below horizon; nautical dawn, when the horizon and a few things become visible but the sun still remains from view some 12 degrees below horizon, until finally the sun is only 6 degrees below horizon. This is the hour before sunrise, known as civil dawn. This is when objects are visible and the sky opens up with light and the day has my full attention. My favourite time of day is when remnants of night linger to catch the sun blushing as it rises from its bed before darkness retreats fully, conceding to daylight. It's a game neither can win at, because at the other end of the day, the roles will be reversed as the sun, even after setting, will reach up with last ditch efforts to hold onto the sky it occupied all those hours until night folds over it and makes it release its hold. It's magic, and it never gets old no matter how often it is played out.

Every day I make the feeble attempt to smell the weather. The best I am able to do is smell the freshness of the cold air and the scent of the soil and rocks after rain. I am not disappointed given it has only been a few days away from my usual life so I haven't had time to hone any instinctual skill, but it has been long enough to recognize the skill is there, just simply out of reach at the moment, waiting to be awoken. There is a thing called olfactory training to awaken that sense we were born with. The technique has you smelling four scents individually for 20 seconds, every day...for months. It isn't surprising I haven't been successful over the course of just four days.

With daylight full on and hours of reflection and pondering behind me, it is time to take up my camp. This morning my tent is still soaked from last night's rain. As I roll it up, I feel the extra weight of it from the water and I am grateful there are no more portages ahead of me. The ground sheet, equally saturated, picks up every pine needle and other tree debris found on the ground and folds so much thicker than when it is dry, I am unable to put it in its carry case. It, too, has added weight.

I carry my gear a bit at a time down the rocky embankment as my water purifies for drinking and for a mug of coffee. My footsteps bite into the gravelly shore, sending stones scattering. I turn my canoe right side up and begin packing it up for the final time.

I enjoy my daily square of dark chocolate. The snap of the chocolate as I break it is satisfying, particularly after three days of soft food. There is a great deal of enjoyment in the few moments it takes to sit in awareness and let it melt in my mouth. Thank goodness I brought it, the trail mix and the three mini bottles of scotch because these items have added such pleasure.

Later, my coffee mug drained, washed out and put away along with everything else, I am ready to head out on the last leg of my solo journey, and while I am excited to return to see Tom and tell him my stories, and revel in the success of completing my trip, I find at the same time, I don't want it to end.

Dip, lift, dip, lift from side to side – drips fall from the paddle back into the lake. I have this movement down to perfection now and I am dry. Thinking back to the first day and how I was soaked the first five minutes into my adventure, this was progress I was pleased with.

I paddled slow but steady, following the contour of the land, watching for rocks and sunken logs, searching beyond the shoreline trees on sentry duty into the forest for any wildlife making their way down for a drink and feeling that everything was right with the world – at least, my world. The trees are shedding last night's rain. Large drops, a compilation of small drops reaching the tip of a leaf, let go and land with a plop on leaves below causing them to dip down and spring back up, appearing like random piano keys being struck by invisible fingers.

No Expiry

This lake hadn't been exclusively mine last night as all the other lakes on my journey, but I may as well have been the only one as no campfires blinked at me from across the lake or anywhere in the distance along the shoreline. Even this morning, I was the only one on the lake as far as I could see.

I rounded the last point of land to where Kiosk campground was located and the bay opened up before me. I could see in the distance a break in the trees and some sandy beach where I would land, and there, standing on the shore, was Tom, and sitting on alert beside him, was Cedar. I could only just make them out. My heart swelled with love. It swelled with the love I had for Tom and it swelled in the knowledge that I was loved. Tom hadn't been overly excited about me doing this trip alone and I know he worried about me out here, yet he supported me every step of the way, suppressing his own feelings about my journey. This is a solid partnership I would never take for granted. I was glad that I had compromised and agreed to take the radio and check in with him daily. It really hadn't been too much to ask of me and I did look forward to talking to him briefly each morning and evening.

As I neared them, Cedar stood up, focusing on my approach. Then, when he was certain, his tail began to wag and he could barely contain himself. I beamed. What a welcome home this was. My grin was wide as I rode up softly on shore, lifting the paddle out of the water for the last time. The dream I carried around for years, the planning I worked on for months, the loop I set out on four days ago, all now complete. I saw the smile in Tom's eyes and nothing needed to be said at all, on this, the very day we got married 44 years ago. Our family unit was back together as it had been, only I felt like a mentally and physically stronger woman than when I left. The wilderness had presented me with some tests, and I had passed them all, strengthening character attributes such as self-confidence, patience, awareness, appreciation, preparedness and acceptance. Doing this solo trip had been so much more than the physical aspect of it.

Together we carried my gear to our campsite where our trailer sat looking like a luxury five star hotel. In his thoughtful manner, Tom had turned the propane hot water heater on anticipating I would want a hot shower when I arrived. I quickly planned my priorities. Carry the canoe back to the base camp office and place it where the rentals are kept, have a shower, put on fresh clothes and have a large mug of tea.

Some campers on either side of us knew I was back and stopped by quickly to congratulate me and thought it was wonderful that I had done this without allowing age to determine my decision. It's true. If we have the ability there is no reason we cannot reach for the things we wish to do, and even if the ability isn't there but we are capable of achieving it through work, then we should feel like there are no barriers to successfully doing anything we want. Ultimately, there is only ourselves to stop us.

The canoe got returned, I had the most luxurious shower I can ever remember having and the tea was heaven in a cup. Other than when I was in the shower, Cedar was lying next to me, his head resting heavily on my foot. I wasn't getting away from him again. At this point I didn't have any other plans, I felt happily satiated, but I could not promise him that I wouldn't do it again in the future.

THE EVER AFTER OR A NEW BEGINNING?

The breeze at dawn has secrets to tell you. Don't go back to sleep ~ Rumi

The day I returned from my trip is hard to explain. Euphoric? Yes. Sorry it was over? Yes. Glad to be back? Yes, to all these things. It was also an instant and automatic shift from nature's time to life amongst others time. While I don't mean to say I stepped out of the canoe and was immediately swept up in a list of "must do's", yet it was an adjustment. Other than singing on the portages to warn bears I was coming through, I hadn't talked at all. I also hadn't had to consider anyone else when deciding what to do next. You develop a rhythm out there as nature quickly takes us back from whence we came. Now there was busy-ness around me and things to do, places to go…all of which were pleasant, but made me giggle to myself at how quickly the barely there sound of my paddle entering the water, pulling, driving my vessel forward, then exiting with a parade of water drops racing after each other to return to the lake, and the smoothness of my motion were already a memory. A past experience. It was nonetheless my experience, and mine alone, which could not be taken away. I am a different person. I have paddled lakes, swam in them, jumped rope on their shores and known them intimately, listened to rapids tripping their way over rocks, gurgling and splashing, tread quietly through forests carrying my canoe overhead, assembled camp, slept out alone in the place that nature's creatures call home, dismantled camp, turned an ear to the winds to listen and laid down on bare rock in the forest to look up to the sky amongst the treetops allowing the sunlight to nourish me.

It isn't a rush I return to. After my leisurely shower and multiple cups of tea at the pace I desire, savouring every sip and thinking how grand life is while at the same time patting my dog, I share with Tom the details of my journey and show him the pictures I took. Later, I relayed my experience with the neighbouring campers on either side who were interested in knowing what it was like out there. It was a lovely post trip experience.

I

As it was our 44th wedding anniversary, we were heading out early on a lengthy drive for a dinner of fish and chips in celebration as planned. For several years we have been here at Kiosk campground for our anniversary and this is what we have come to do every year.

The three of us, Tom, Cedar and I, find ourselves in downtown Mattawa, sitting in an otherwise empty parking lot of a hotel/restaurant awaiting our take-out order. We are facing the Ottawa River, a waterway used by aboriginal people for more than 6,000 years. Many of its portages still remain much the same as they were during the time of the Voyageurs. I conjure up visions of large, muscular men with lots of facial hair and woolen caps pulled over their heads, digging their paddles deep into the water, all of them synchronized, powering down the river. Mattawa means "river with walls that echo its current" in Algonkian language, and as I look across to the other side onto a vertical and heavily forested slope of conifers that line its banks as far as I can see, I understand how this name was arrived at. Twenty minutes later our dinner is ready for pick-up and we head to the town park located a little downriver to enjoy it. Afterwards, I take pictures trying to capture the ruggedness of the area while Tom and Cedar wait patiently. I am still in "commune with nature" mode, so I take my time.

It is dark as we travel the quiet dirt road back to the campground, once again leaving the world of cell service and amenities behind. Our headlights reach the shoulder, illuminating metal warning signs on the guard rails meant to stop you from catapulting down the embankment into the river below. It is along here that we see him, a big bull moose running on the forest side of the guard rails, on what narrow strip of ground there is before the edge. He kept going, as do we so as not to frighten him, or much more likely, not to make him angry or feel threatened. Tom figures he was making his way down to the river when we came upon him. All I could think of was that I had been out in the wilderness for four days, in prime moose territory as I watchfully paddled through tall grasses and reeds, and yet I hadn't seen one, but on my first day back, I see one on a road next to guard rails. Funny how it goes sometimes.

A few days later, Tom and I were out on a drive again into Mattawa to pick up some supplies, and as we sometimes do, we headed off to look at what was once Moosehead Lodge, where I had lived with my grandparents and great-grandparents. Aside from the fact it is now a private cottage, the long road in has newer laneways which branch off leading to other cottages that have been built over the decades since I left. We always stop at the end of the driveway at the lodge where an old, weathered sign of a moose head still hangs nailed to a tree, a nod to the place's past. I look at the whelping shed where I used to play with the hunting dogs and I remember quite clearly the time I accidentally locked myself in there and lay crying out for help at the floor level opening blocked with chicken wire so the puppies wouldn't get out until finally my grandmother heard me wailing and came to rescue me. There is the window on the second story of the house which I am sure was my bedroom where on summer nights the sound of whip-poor-wills in the forest would lull me to sleep. I think of the time I was supposed to be having an afternoon nap and instead climbed out the window at the end of the hallway onto the roof to play with the rooster weather vane. I got caught when my great-grandmother saw my shadow on the ground from the kitchen below, alerting her to the mischief I was up to.

It is time to go, but maybe one time when we come here, there will be someone home and with luck they will allow us to see the inside.

We are on our way out. Tom stops and lets me walk a bit on the road that winds through the forest so I can bask in memories. I walk it slowly as he stays back and edges the vehicle forward every now and then. I remember walking with my grandfather on this road, pulling a sled, I was almost four years old. We went into the forest, trekking through the deep snow to get a Christmas tree. While my grandfather chopped the tree, and the sun began to sink low in the sky, I began to worry. I asked him how we were going to find our way home? It never occurred to me we would simply follow our footprints out. Before he could answer me, some crows began to caw as they moved through the trees, no doubt heading to their nighttime roosting spot, glossy black feathers in a white environment. He turned to me and said, "The crows will show us the way home." I've never forgotten this and I think it is part of the reason why I love crows so much. I often repeat this to my husband when we are on a hike, as he often does to me, too. It's a story that sticks.

Eventually I am back in the truck and we are leaving history behind. We hardly get going again and ahead of us a healthy looking black bear appears on the road, moving lithely regardless its bulky size this time of year. It sees us, lifts its head and bolts without effort up a rocky cliff, its strong limbs powering it upwards until it is out of sight. We are shocked at the ease with which it has disappeared over the top of the almost vertical rocks. It makes me have even more respect for the animal. Again, I find myself thinking how I had not seen a bear on my trip, yet here one is, on the outskirts of a town. I decide there is a lot less anxiety seeing a bear from the safety of a vehicle than it would have been at my campsite when I was alone in the middle of nowhere. It's all a matter of perspective.

I realize it is complete. I had ached spiritually for almost five years to do this trip not even realizing that it was a need not based on being victorious in the quest itself, but to be bound once again to this land that I had lost connection with. Fear and doubt had plagued me in those first years of desire when I felt I was incapable of making it happen. I was a 65 year old woman. Society's narrative says older people can't do things such as this. We need to be careful so as not to hurt our frail selves. Anyway, weren't goals like these something only people with strong character could pull off? As my desire evolved into something which must be done, I had realized that no one else could say anything or do anything to make this happen for me. I very simply had to do it myself. I was the only one with the control to make the shift from a dream to reality, and I had finally done just that. Me.

Many weeks later, the blood surging through my veins since that final day when I took my paddle out of the water for the last time still feels electrified and has me on a continual high. I still can't quite believe I have done it. It all started with a spark, that ignited into a flame that burned brighter and brighter until it could no longer be extinguished. Thinking hadn't been enough. I had to take action. In retrospect, it seems as though it should have been innate. It is empowering, nonetheless, to have this new found wisdom by way of first-hand experience and know that it is as simple as taking that first step and continuing forward, steadfastly and with confidence

I sigh with contentment when asked if I will do such a trip again. Possibly. I don't really know for certain. For now, I am satiated. I have completed what I set out to do, and it became so much more than I ever could have anticipated. Not only did I transform my dream into reality and in so doing change my outlook on life, I also came away with something important to share that society needs to hear. And that is – if you have the ability, whatever it is that you dream of doing, age is irrelevant. We have no expiry.

EPILOGUE

A year later and I am back. Back at Kioshkokwi Lake and it is as beautiful as ever. Now when I look out across the lake, I see more than I used to when I had only my imagination to tell me what lay beyond the lakes, forests, hills and marshes. I can visualize it exactly, at least in the area of last year's solo canoe trip.

One night after dinner, as the sun is contemplating the drop behind the treeline, I go out for a solo paddle. The winds of the day have abated and the lake has settled into a calm where clearly visible ever expanding rings on the surface indicate where a fish has leapt beyond its natural boundaries to feed. I don't have a destination in mind when I leave the shores of the campground, particularly with the impending darkness. I am just happy to be out on the water in my canoe.

The paddle slips smoothly, silently into the water in the way I had come to expect when the two of us work together.

Then suddenly I don't care that it is getting dark. I know my way here, and before I have time to reconsider, I am heading with intention down the lake, and I know exactly where I am going.

Eventually I see it, the spot where I camped on the last day of my four day solo journey into the backcountry. I recognize the trees, the shoreline and the spot where I turned my canoe upside-down for the night. I get emotional then.

I think about the date. It's September 15th and it is one year to the day that I spent the night on this spot. How is it that I happened to end up here right on the very day one year later without planning it? Is there something more at work here than coincidence? Was my experience so deep that my subconscious remembers when I do not? Those days out there alone, paddling the lakes, trekking the portages with my canoe and all my gear, becoming irreversibly entwined with nature – I became something different. I can't be the same person I was. When we realize our dreams we become fulfilled, when we don't reach for those dreams we lose our vigour.

Reluctantly, I turn the canoe to head back and as I face west, what I see moves me and I am mesmerized. The sun is no longer visible but there lingers a heated orange-yellow glow peaking between violet-grey clouds which spill onto the lake turning the surface into threads of spun gold, vibrating and shimmering in the fading light, and it feels like a gift specifically for me and suddenly there are tears of gratitude I have no control over.

Last year, when I returned home following my trip, I was on a high…for months. I searched for a way to commemorate this achievement that was so important to me and for about ten seconds, I considered a tattoo. After acknowledging that a tattoo wasn't for me, I decided to find an artist who worked with silver, could understand my vision, and have a ring made - something that would signify my accomplishment that I could wear as a reminder - something that could be passed down in the family. After all, one couldn't pass down a tattoo.

My search led me to Teri of Silver Suspensions in British Columbia. Over the months, we worked together and came up with a true representation of what I wanted this piece to say. Three stones in my ring, all of them Canadian, tell the story. The largest, a B.C. ocean stone of varied blues with a few flecks of bronze, represents the lakes I paddled, with the bronze looking like the autumn leaves found in the water along the shorelines this time of year. Next, a small sunstone, a bronze orange representing the land I portaged over. The third stone is a tiny diamond that adds a touch of sparkle and balance to the ring and represents the fact you can shine at any age. The setting around the stones is surrounded by branches, all finely textured to look like woodgrain, and so, too, is the band, with branches along the top and bottom all the way around. The band itself is wide, which allows for other important additions which further my story. A waning moon stands for the nights I spent out there in nature's hold, a canoe wraps itself around the back of the band, the vessel of my journey, and a set of legs walking is me portaging through the forests, up hills and along rivers as I realized my dream. On the inside of the ring, behind the setting, is the inscription 'Algonquin Park' along with the dates of my trip.

How have I changed during this past year since embarking on this solo canoe trip? I listen better. I believe I rush less. I am no longer fearful of the forest at night and as a woman, now age 66, I am more confident than ever that I can do what I set out to do and I am driven to encourage you, that you, too, can do hard things…things you have desired and dreamed of but never got to do, either due to fear or lack of confidence in ability. We need only be creative in planning it out, breaking it down into manageable parts until the whole is before us, and then taking action and doing it. It doesn't matter what it is, but we need to do this in order to be true to ourselves. Life is a gift, growing older is a privilege and we owe it to ourselves to stay in the game and make the most of it.

No Expiry

Have you ever stood where the silences brood,
And vast the horizons begin,
At the dawn of the day to behold far away
The goal you would strive for and win?
Yet ah! In the night when you gain to the height,
With the vast pool of heaven star-spawned,
Afar and agleam, like a valley of dream,
Still mocks you a Land of Beyond

~Robert Service

Sheila Nollert

Made in the USA
Monee, IL
16 February 2024

53620882R00069